12/95

Jane;
from
Diana
Sept. 8, 1987

LOVING LIFE

LOVING
LIFE

Helen Hayes

WITH

Marion Glasserow Gladney

DOUBLEDAY & COMPANY, INC.
GARDEN CITY, NEW YORK
1987

Library of Congress Cataloging-in-Publication Data
Hayes, Helen, 1900–
    Loving life.
    I. Gladney, Marion Glasserow. II. Title.
PN2287.H35A5 1987   814'.52   86-29244
ISBN: 0-385-23903-3

ACKNOWLEDGMENTS

Without the facile fingers and infallible memories of Andrea Klein and Ani Ardhaldjian this project would have gotten buried under a mountain of reference material or, worse, been rendered irretrievable in a state-of-the-art (art?) devil instrument, the personal computer.

Contents

Introduction

A quick look at the Contents may cause you to wonder whether these are subjects for an actress. Quite frankly, to be even halfway proficient in my trade, one must be somewhat of a Peeping Tom and Renaissance person. Asking myself questions is one sure way of getting satisfactory answers. It fascinates me to observe the rhythm that brings people together and the designs and ambitions that keep them apart.

What are the changes and innovations in the national culture? What is our sense of the future and the past? What disciplines, restraints, and decisions must be contemplated? Every aspect of life, art, science, and social change has a bearing on my private life and on my craft. This book is a panoramic view of the world around me, as I see it—matters that do or should concern everyone. If we could only resolve them, we would surely improve the quality of our existence. We have the capacity to make deserts bloom—or to make deserts. Science is providing answers with such phenomenal speed that philosophy has lost track of the questions.

Life is a rehearsal, in many ways. From the French, *répétition* is more to the point. That is what we do in life, repeat, again and again—mistakes and lessons, problems and solutions, promises and regrets, victories and defeats. We are amateurs trying to act like seasoned veterans without ever having a look at the script. At dawn we rehearse the day; at night we write the critique. The most challenging scene is the finale, for then there is no curtain call, no reprise, and no *deus ex machina* entering to resolve the plot.

I have retired from the stage and from most other forms of expressing my feelings, hopes, questions, fears, joys, doubts, and cautions. That leaves the printed page—the most indulgent of all means of communicating. Paper and pen never contradict me, doubt me, correct me, sneer at me, ignore or deprecate me. If I so choose, they applaud, laugh, cry, or gasp on cue and never fail to make contact with, if not an impact on, my audience. Thus, permit me to zigzag through my mental file of concerns—and bits and pieces of remembrances.

LOVING LIFE

Psycho-Logic

I went to a psychoanalyst—once. My husband, Charles MacArthur, was having a minor nervous breakdown. Writer's block. At some point in their career, it happens to all of them. The well is frozen over. He was desperate and the whole thing was getting out of hand. I was trying to cope. He refused the advice of his doctor to see a "head shrinker," as he put it. Meantime, he got an attack of shingles and all kinds of things happened to him. So, they sent me to the psychoanalyst. I wanted to be told how to help Charlie more efficiently and not continue the mistakes I was sure I was making. I needed guidance. So what was I given? Just what I get everywhere: "You do too much for people. You're too good." I'm so tired of hearing that about me. I never went back.

If you've never been to a psychoanalyst yourself, you have certainly seen enough celluloid versions of therapy sessions to have a good idea of what goes on. There's always that box of tissues prominently displayed. The patient talks a lot, his eyes roaming around the room. The analyst leans back in a swivel chair, surrounded by dangerously leaning stacks of books, and smokes incessantly while staring at the ceiling, not saying much. He supposedly listens intently, making mental notes, which you're sure are of great significance. When the phone interrupts the wildly expensive fifty minutes allotted to your troubles, the lost time is never added on, nor is the broken train of thought reestablished. Actually, what is going on is not psychoanalysis but self-analysis. The anguished patient hears himself speak about problems or avoids talking about them. The best the doctor can do is to encourage this self-examination with an occasional prod.

A cheaper way to find out what's troubling you is to keep a diary. *For My Eyes Only* is the title of your book. Be sure to use a bound notebook or diary with blank pages, and promise yourself never to tear out a page. Oh sure, next month some of what you wrote looks crazy—even to you. But isn't that the point? You will find out that what hurt you, angered you, frightened you wasn't worth these exaggerated emotions. You will get to know your thoughts and have the chance to reexamine them, in retrospect, to better understand yourself, as well as the people who populate your life. Once you have put a thought on paper, you have it in your hand—to study, to improve, to discard, and most important, to forgive yourself.

Have you had any unpleasant thoughts today? Probably more than once. Most likely, thoughts that depress or disturb you are old, familiar enemies that have been hanging around in your head for a long time. You allow them to enter and make no effort to stop them, and then permit them to create havoc with your mental outlook. It is not beyond your control to screen out useless, negative thinking. Psychologists can teach you how to readjust your thinking process in a matter of minutes. The first step is to make yourself aware of these disruptive thoughts, usually self-directed and self-deprecating. Once you have learned to recognize them and can indicate to the therapist that such a thought is crossing your mind, he shouts "STOP." After a very short time, you learn to shout a silent "STOP" to yourself.

Would you allow someone to say to you: "You can't do anything right!"? Of course not. Then why talk yourself down like that? Make an inventory of the detrimental thoughts with which you aggravate or punish yourself. Substitute positive thoughts or pleasant images in their place. The urge to propagate the negative soon abates and constructive thoughts take over. Don't lament: "My husband never appreciates my cooking." Say, instead: "Who cares! *I* like my cooking." Or, "Of course he does, but perhaps not all the time. So be it." To constantly reiterate what's wrong, unpleasant, or frightening is absolutely of no use. Say "STOP" every time you place a barrier in the path of personal contentment. Concentrate on a pleasant fantasy or a positive thought to squelch those devilish mental traps. If you allow destructive thought processes to dominate your life, you deny yourself every chance of happiness and productiveness. Thought-stopping is a most handy device whenever you find yourself mentally whining or wrapping yourself in a useless hair shirt.

Mental stress is a much misunderstood concept. We read the sports pages and find out that a marathon runner collapsed from cardiac arrest. We chat with a neighbor and hear of an unexpected death. Too much stress, they say. Time for a checkup. Blood pressure reading is up and we're told it's due to excessive stress; then what? Calm down, slow down, slim down, sit down. And worry. But that's not going to help any more than "Stress Formula" vitamin pills.

Can stress be cured? Avoided? What *is* stress, anyway? It's the body's physical, mental, and chemical response to things that frighten, excite, confuse, endanger, or irritate. The word itself means "to draw tight"—a sensation that prepares us for action: fighting, fleeing, deciding. Without it, we never would have made it out of the jungle. Stress is caused by everything to which we can affix the word "problem," but also by success and by fun, newness, challenge, and sport. Eliminate all stress and our lives would be about as exciting as a perpetual Sunday afternoon nap. Stress creates the demands that cause us to excel, make us interesting, and keep us interested. The body reacts to stressors with a variety of chemical changes, which, in turn, produce dramatic physical and mental changes. We are not programmed to be made ill by it, but challenged and stimulated to take appropriate action. These changes enable us to react quickly when in danger, to fight if necessary, to muster great strength if needed, to run with greater speed, or to make logical decisions. In the absence of dinosaurs and erupting volcanoes, decide what may be too stressful in your life and what is a prod to achievement. Teach yourself to relax. Ignore the clock at times and take a break. Permit yourself some self-love.

We may be living in the twentieth century, in resplendent sophistication. But deep down, most of us find ourselves still in the Stone Age of superstition. We knock on wood and deprecate our successes. We fear that tooting our own horn will bring down the wrath of the gods. Why are we so afraid to savor what's good in life, accomplishments, joys, and benefits? Many people truly believe that adversity is justly deserved, perhaps for merely having enjoyed ourselves. Psychologist Dr. Susan Schenkel suggests that we may feel guilt for receiving bounty, that unacceptable behavior must have been the source of it. Reaction of friends and relations to our good fortune may be one of the underlying reasons for such unreasonable thoughts. Very often they react strangely, almost with misgiving, disapproval, or unaccountable silence. Do we or don't we deserve unexpected or dearly-worked-for successes and rewards? The price we fear the gods will exact from us to balance joy and pain equally has been termed "cosmic equity." Women are especially susceptible to these self-effacing attitudes. Was it ability, just luck, or fate that got her the raise or made the angel cake rise? Megan Marshall "discovered that fear of the ephemeral nature of good fortune seems to be exacerbated in women by a belief that anything won, even by skill, could be lost by a single slipup."* (Slam the oven door and the cake collapses!) Men are, perhaps, not quite so vulnerable to a let-down. But then, they are geared to parade their pride before women, who fear to do the same in return.

---

* *The Cost of Loving: Women and the New Fear of Intimacy,* Putnam, New York, 1984

Frame of Mind

Everyday mundane conversation, quite often, is deceptively difficult. Ask a question, make a comment, state an observation, or give suggestions, and something goes wrong. What causes the tension, the lack of unwarranted responses? Why the negative response or, worse, the silence? Much of what goes wrong between people, especially those who live together, starts with words. If you observe carefully, you might come to the conclusion that the two actors in such a play are reading from two different scripts. We have preconceived responses in mind when we speak. What is said to us, we assume, also requires an expected response. "Do you like this color nail polish on me?" Does she hide in that silly question the fact that he has not noticed the new shade of pink? Is "Mmm" enough of an answer? Would she be hurt if he said: "The other color was fine with me" or "I never liked it?"

As we speak, we look for the effect our words are having, or we imagine it. If the listener's eyes wander, there is little doubt that the response won't be what we hoped for. If we plan to have a fine conversation, must we stick to only subjects of interest to the other person? It might help, but not enough. Most people think only they themselves can get into the depth of their own thoughts; any attempt by an outsider will fall flat.

"How are you?" is a greeting, not an invitation to unburden your problems. George Kaufman said: A bore is someone who, when you ask "how are you?" tells you.

Speaker of the House Sam Rayburn was of the opinion that the three most important words in the English language are: Wait A Minute. No Northerner could have made that the cadence of his life. Starting on a career path to the top step by step as a cotton picker, as he did, allows for plenty of time to develop a personal philosophy. Think what it means to "wait a minute"—before you act, before you react, before you speak. You can change your mind, or make up your mind in that time. (Notice how many thoughts go through your head while you are reading this.) Sam Rayburn was a middle-of-the-road Democrat whose knowledge and diplomacy kept him securely in the office of Speaker of the House longer than any of his predecessors. He contributed a unique prestige to parliamentary leadership. Infinite patience may have been the substructure.

If you know the many variants of "wait a minute," well, then you can hit a fine golf stroke; you'll avoid many arguments; reticence will keep your weight down; patience will make you a better parent. Waiting a minute lets you think things through with care. Or, to be sure of your ground, you take time to look it up. A minute's hesitation, when tempted to buy, can help balance your budget. It steadies your equilibrium—mind and body. It can prevent a verbal wound and calm your nerves. It may make you seem very wise, and it helps you see truth and beauty unexpectedly. It substitutes for useless words and emotions and opens you to much that might otherwise have escaped you. To wait a minute puts many things in proper perspective, sharpens what might be blurred, softens uncalled-for harshness. We have nothing so much as time. Why do we rush through it so energetically as though our thoughts, our actions, would be of no value a minute from now?

If you are a gardener, like me, you know not to replant the same vegetables in last year's spot, and you enrich the soil generously with appropriate nutrients. Many a philosopher has used nature as an analogy for the human mind, as did the famed eighteenth-century English portrait painter, Sir Joshua Reynolds. He thought of the mind as "barren soil, soil that is soon exhausted and will produce no crop unless it is continually fertilized and enriched with foreign matter." It is interesting that he thought of mental stimulation as "foreign matter," material that comes not from within, but from sources outside ourselves. How true that is! Recycling our thoughts, rehashing experiences, rehearsing old wounds only results in mental stagnation. If we don't open the doors and windows of our minds, nothing will flower within.

"The mind requires both change and input; clearly the input must be new. This doesn't mean that the material must be new to the rest of the world; it means it must be new to you."* You don't have to sight a new comet and have it named after you. You could just go outside, look at the constellations, and learn to recognize one other than the Big Dipper. We use only the most infinitesimal part of our brains (just as we breathe with only ten percent of our lung capacity). There is no such thing as a partially open mind. What holds us back from developing up to the maximum potential is that we think we know our limitations. We put restraints on ourselves, far more inhibiting than any we would allow others to inflict on us. Bottling up our thoughts can only result in a Molotov cocktail.

In the opinion of George Jean Nathan, the critic, "no man can think clearly when his fists are clenched." There is a good deal of controversy about handling anger. Is it good to vent it, to release it? Can it be constructive, physically and emotionally, or do we harm ourselves and those around us when we explode our grievances, shrapnel-fashion? The pendulum is swinging, once again. Letting it all hang out may not do any good, after all. Sustaining an angry mood is so tempting, some do it indefinitely. Does holding under

the feelings of anger cause ulcers? Heart attacks? Head-
aches? Will it make you anorexic or obese? "Talking out an
emotion does not reduce it; it rehearses it."† Isn't that what
people are doing when they rail against the boss or co-
worker in the washroom and against their roommate or
spouse at lunch? When we think of being "livid," we forget
that it means ashen, drained of blood, pale with anger.
What we lose when we lose our temper is the blood supply
to the brain, which impairs our thinking process. Fury is a
storm that blows out your mind.

Where do you suppose the phrase "flying off the handle"
comes from? Perhaps it has always meant that, with uncontrolled anger, we dig our own graves so furiously that the
spade flies off the handle and we end up holding the dirty
end of the stick. Philosophers throughout the ages have
addressed the subject of anger. But only now, with medical
attention focused on cause and effect, do we begin to understand that when we lose our temper, we gain nothing. On
the contrary, we damage our health.

Anger has become a universal problem, visible in just
about every person, group, and nation. We are being pro-
voked, almost continuously, by personal contact, public information, and international events. This is a frustrating
society. "Remember that anger reaction is built into the
human organism as a response to life-or-death confrontations."‡ Some studies of anger advocate venting it as a
relief and normalizing process. But more recent attitudes by
psychologists declare this to be less salutary, perhaps even
damaging or habit-forming. "Expressing anger is a form of
public littering; a thermostat stuck always at hot."‡ Rage
has its beginning in infancy; the baby resents its dependency and fears neglect. The fear of abandonment may well
start in the birth process itself. Separation, what an awesome thing that is. How angry do you get when the gas
station attendant neglects to rush back after the pump clicks
off and the "umbilical cord" has ceased fueling your car?
"Whenever an individual finds himself in a position of de-

pendency, he will recast the current reality in terms of the helpless phase of childhood, evoking all the urgency and volatility of that earlier state."‡

"Count to ten"—just what I always say.

Grandparents Are History

When General Eisenhower was president of Columbia University, General Omar Bradley and I were given honorary degrees. Bradley was so elated that day because he had just had a new grandson. He told me, "Now I know why we have children, so we can have grandchildren." The honor that was being paid him by that great university sort of faded into the background.

Social scientists apparently never run out of new groups to study. The latest is grandparents. That's no surprise when you consider that at the turn of the century only three million Americans lived beyond their sixty-fifth year. Today, more than 24 million make up this venerable group of elders. Just what is their role in the three- and four-generation family and in society? Do they want to be considered living symbols or active participants? Both, I would hope. "By simply being there, grandparents perform a valuable function," says the author of a research book on the subject. "Their mere existence is an expression of family continuity. They serve as an anchor of stability. They are a link to the past, not just to members of a particular family, but to members of a previous social order."* They function as a connection with humanity, with history.

My own two grandchildren were lost to me during their formative years. Their parents' separation made them inaccessible to me for a number of years. One doesn't hear of "alienation of affection" as a cause for divorce so often now. But it frequently is the result for grandparents and grandchildren. Early intimacy has no substitutes. Last year, these two beautiful young adults came to visit me and then escorted me to the White House when I was honored with the Medal of Freedom. I had been working at home on a family album. All the photographs of the family—their baby pictures; their father, grandfather, and their aunt, my darling Mary; Nyack and Cuernavaca—a historic overview with no particular plan in mind. I was timid about pushing it on them. But, subliminally, I suppose there was method in my having "left" it on the coffee table when young Charlie and Mary came to visit. They literally fell on it with such avidity. They sat over it for days, sharing their youth, their history, their connection to the family.

Getting better and older is that boy, that man closest to my heart, my son James. Now that he has acquired his second family, he is a *new* father, a *new* husband in every sense of the word. At the age of forty-eight, he has an infant son who should have been my great-grandson, of course. (His first born, Charlie, is already twenty-seven). It is no less miraculous to be the gaga grandma, once again, to this wonderful new being. Yet, I'm just a smidgen jealous of my friends who have attained that venerated, hyphenated status. (I have pleaded with young Charlie to settle down, but he delights in reminding me that I always advised him to live life to the fullest as long as possible.) Proof that later is lovelier is in watching James now. He is getting so much more out of this new baby and taking so much more trouble and interest than when first he was a young father of twenty-two. He walks around with this child on his back, packs up the little family in the van with enough equipment to criss-

cross the country. He is just in heaven as a father now. And I
don't think that is unique.

Many of the ills of our time can probably be attributed to
rootlessness. People scatter, each unit following its own
star. We end up apart from each other. The telephone,
contrary to campaign slogans, is not a cohesive force. A
family unit that lacks the anchor of its own past cannot easily
maintain its equilibrium. The presence of grandparents can
exert a calming influence, not only during times of transi-
tion, but in a continuation of stability. Sadly, it is the high
divorce rate that draws researchers' attention to the importance of grandparents. Many are forced into positions they
did not anticipate. Either they lose their status as grandparents, through separation, or they take on the task of parenting once more. Many of them never knew their own grandparents well, if at all. They had no role models for their
current situation. Whatever great revelations and wisdom
social science sleuths will discover about today's grandparents, I hope they won't preach to us, with such advice as:
"Don't preach. Don't participate. Don't say, when I was
your age. Don't." Yes, do. By all means, do. Tell, teach,
admonish, love, spoil, listen, listen, listen. The children's
parents and teachers are busy, bossy, impatient, tense, wor-
ried, harassed, and helpless. They'll appreciate an adult
who pays attention to them—one at a time.

I've been a grandmother since I was thirty-five years old.
No, no—I wasn't all that precocious. It was as Queen Victoria, in *Victoria Regina,* that I played the part of the world's
most famous grandmother. But even long before that, I was
familiar with the power of grandmotherhood. My Graddy
Hayes had a monumental influence on my life. She lived
with us, and I can only pity all those children who don't have
such a wonderful link to their own history living in close
proximity during their formative years. I know I would not
be who I am today if my Graddy had not touched me, taught
me, tended to me every day while I was growing up. If you
have grandchildren, how do you communicate with them?
By phone? Letters? Christmas cards and gifts? What do they

get to know about you, your history, which is theirs, too, your life, your beliefs?

One thing most older folks have in common are thoughts about what we wish we had done better, especially with our children. Well, it's not possible to be perfect, to go back and undo, do over, do more. The lucky ones have grandchildren to whom they can be responsive parent figures, which they failed to be to their own children. During the years we raise our children, we are totally absorbed in building our lives, careers, homes, and economic standards. In retrospect, most fathers feel they didn't spend enough time with their sons and daughters. They were too occupied with making a better life for them; they missed most of the life there was to be lived.

For teenagers, a grandparent can be just the one to further their intellectual and human development. They can be closer than parents and children. A growing girl can talk more easily to her grandmother about her personal problems than to her mother. A grandfather brings a different perspective to his grandson's career planning or financial situation. He can give advice without preachment. He can concentrate on him. Neither one needs to prove anything. The older man or woman is recognized by the searching youngster as having the time, interest, money, experience, and patience to accept facts and help develop options. Foreign-born grandparents shouldn't overlook the opportunity of passing on ethnic and regional traditions and knowledge. The "generation between" was too busy—learning to run with the pack—to see much value in retaining differences. It's sad when foreign surnames are Americanized, losing the melody or ruggedness, the flavor of their origin. Grandparents can learn about life today from children. They are the world, proclaims the song. They are the ones who'll make a brighter day.

Mark Van Doren calls grandchildren "children once removed" in a poem that is on the first page of a delightful book. *Grandparents' Houses* is a brief anthology of just fifteen poems representing many cultures, among them Zuni, Japa-

nese, Chinese, Hebrew, American, and German. Some are
folk poems, others are the works of well-known poets. All
reflect the universal love and reverence we have for our
parents' parents. Grandparents, then, are parents once removed, but in some ways closer. Easier to love and be loved
by. Here's a sample poem from this charmingly illustrated
book:

> Grandmother, you gave me the wealth of detail.
> You taught me to love grass and moss,
> ants and butterflies . . .
> You gave me my first trees and my first sunset,
> mushroom hunts and the bliss of long walks.

Other poets sing of the white, white kitchen; the smell of
October, of onions, soap, wet clay. In "The Legacy," a
grandfather is remembered:

> Grandfather never went to school,
> spoke only a few words of English, a quiet man;
> when he talked, talked about simple things.
> Planting corn or about the weather,
> sometimes about herding sheep as a child.
> One day pointed to the four directions,
> taught me their names
> El Norte, Poniente, Oriente, El Sud.
> He spoke their names as if they were one of only a
> handful of things
> a man needed to know.
> Now I look back
> only two generations removed,
> realize I am nothing but a poor fool
> who went to college
> trying to find my way back
> to the center of the world
> where grandfather stood
> that day

I'm sure I'm not alone in remembering, so vividly, the
hands of my grandmother.

On the side of a city building is a huge poster from the U. S. Treasury Department. It really displeases me. A grandmotherly lady with a friendly face, clutching her purse. A group of teenagers in the background, slouching on the steps of a tenement. The headline proclaims: "Now that I have direct deposit, I'm not so popular with the boys anymore." Nothing could be more damaging to the relationship between young and old, and to the self-image of both. An advertisement like this breeds fear and contempt; it fires the anger that members of each age group feel toward the other and against their own, often helpless, status. Here's an example: An old lady who asked a passerby to help her to the post office was angry with the swiftly revolving door, angry with the dim illumination, angry with the too-high stand-up desk, and even angry with the good Samaritan whom she asked for help. Let's have a new set of twenty-four-sheet posters on our billboards around the country, messages that will broadcast what's *right* with the world, before we will need crash helmets and bulletproof vests. Old people, left alone, suffer in silence. Young people, alienated from the world, suffer aggressively. When the post office security guard was asked to further help the old woman address and mail her letter, he seemed glad to be roused out of his stupor of boredom and uselessness. His smile and his eagerness to render a service set up good vibes among the embarrassed folks, who had been hearing the angry old lady sound off. And she actually beamed, even as the guard refused a tip.

From Preppies we get Yuppies and, sometimes, Puppies —who eventually become Grumpies! What that translates to is that our educated offspring soon grow into "Young Upwardly Mobile Professionals" (Yuppies). Some consider themselves *"Poor* Upwardly Mobile Professionals" (Puppies) when they compare their status with that of their parents at the same age. Now these parents have been dubbed "Grumpies" (by a publication that should know better!). That somewhat sour-sounding acronym stands for "Grownup Mature Persons," namely the over-fifties. Let's put a halt to that one before it deteriorates into "Oafs"—"Older Active Folks." Listen my fellow maturians, we have the power! As a group, the elderly are a potent and growing financial source.

The day we lisp, "I'm goin' on three," we become aware of wanting to be—to be what? Older. Mature. Independent. Responsible for ourselves. That never really changes. We have a certain pride about the age we are, even though we may experience a mild depression at the round-numbered birthdays. Editors, columnists, and writers are always looking for new angles in demographics. They're bored with the college crowd, sated on divorce statistics, talked-out about women's issues, and not sure how much more we want to know about the new baby boom. The new category of interest to demographers is the mature population. Maturians. "The consumers of the future" (why future?) are named "Sippies" by *Working Woman* magazine. "Senior Independent Pioneers (Sippies) will soon control U.S. buying power." You like that acronym? It sounds a bit too frail and wimpy. How about "Aimies," instead? *A* for active, *I* for independent, *M* for maturian—fifty-five to eighty and beyond. "Aimies" reminds me of the French for like, and for love, too. Demographers call the years from sixty to seventy-five "extended middle age." By the year 2000, over 30 million Americans will be "Aimies." The manufacturer who wants his share of that market should get to know it well. "They already command almost thirty percent of all discretionary funds." They come by their purchasing power through hard work, stringent savings, and prudent investments and insurance. They know the value of goods and use discretion in spending. I don't think they'll spend forty-eight dollars on a pair of plastic earrings.

Grandparents represent one other vitally important chapter in a child's life. They die. Now and then, the front page brings a touching photo, such as that of the artificial-heart recipient kissing his grandchild the day before surgery. Saying goodbye? Just in case . . . ? How many people would devoutly love to have this privilege? But most institutions won't allow it—except for front-page celebrities, perhaps. As surely as we are all born, we all die. But that fact is still treated like a closely guarded secret. How many people have actually seen death? Except for medical professionals, most younger people haven't witnessed dying. And children, certainly never. Why? In our cultural background are the "neighbor ladies" who assembled in the bereaved household to wash and prepare the body. The old women sewed the shroud; young men cut the boards and joined the casket; other men dug the grave; and children helped prepare food for the wake. That was *life*. It preceded condolence cards.

Why do we persist in treating death like a nightmare? (Don't look; it'll go away.) Are we beginning to believe that life can be extended indefinitely? Emil Brunner, the Swiss theologian, thought eternal "continuance of this life—that would, perhaps, be Hell." If we were not so ignorant about death and dying, we would not fear old age so much, would we? In *Leaves of Grass*, Walt Whitman wrote: "Youth, large, lusty, loving; youth, full of grace, force, fascination. Do you know that Old Age may come to you with equal grace, force, fascination?" To me, this lovely poem emphasizes that we should live as fully, as long, as ardently as we possibly can— not because we're afraid of stopping, but because we've got so much yet to do. We don't have to cave in at some arbitrary point on the calendar. But we should, as a society, accept the simple logic and dignity of death.

Nat, the old man in Herb Gardner's play *I'm Not Rappaport*, has a penchant for adopting a variety of pseudopersonalities—quick character changes to keep himself on the edge of life. It's a game he plays to maintain his sanity— perhaps also to elude and confound the celestial stagehand who's getting ready to lower the curtain on his life. He spends his waking hours on a park bench. He is old, independent, imaginative, and a thorn in his sidekick, old black Midge. Nat loves taking on the whole world—one at a time. In the following confrontation, he makes verbal mincemeat out of the chairman of a cooperative apartment house, who is conspiring to relieve old Midge of his duties as superintendent, a maneuver which would also put Midge out of his basement apartment. Nat hits young, upwardly mobile Danforth where it hurts:

You are so extraordinarily ordinary, because there are so many of you now. You collect old furniture, old cars, old pictures, everything old but old people. Bad souvenirs, they talk too much. Even quiet, they tell you too much, they look like the future and you don't want to know. Who are these people, these oldies, this strange race; they're not my type, put them with their own kind—a building, a town—put them someplace. You idiots, don't you know? One day you too will join this weird tribe. Yes, Mr. Chairman, you will get old; I hate to break the news. And if you're frightened now, you'll be terrified then. The problem's not that life is short, but that it's very long; so you better have a policy. Here we are. Look at us. We're the coming attractions. And, as long as you're afraid of it, you'll be afraid of us, you will want to hide us or make us hide from you. You're dangerous. Don't you understand? The old people, they're the survivors, they know something, they haven't just stayed late to ruin your party. The very old, they are miracles like the just-born; close to the end is precious; like close to the beginning."†

* *Grandparenthood*, Dr. Vern Bengtson and Joan Robertson, Sage, Beverly Hills, California, 1985
† *I'm Not Rappaport* (excerpted by permission)

Salad Days

Things you're sure to encounter in coffee shops. Dishes, which are "star war" proof (that's why they can be thrown from six feet into a bin). And a salad (ordered or included) —invariably a wedge of ice-cold, ice-green iceberg lettuce with a dab of something oily-pink that the Russians may yet consider the ultimate provocation! How did a food so gruesome as iceberg lettuce become the all-American favorite choice as the green accompaniment to a meal? Shakespeare reminds us of his "salad days, when I was green in judgment, cold in blood." What you should do with iceberg lettuce, in cold blood, is sauté it briefly with onions and zucchini and never, never serve it raw with Russian dressing. And don't think you're killing the nutrients, because that particular head of lettuce is virtually empty of vitamins A and C, calcium, iron, and potassium.

Iceberg lettuce, also known as Great Lakes or Crisphead, has one-tenth the vitamin A of endive. Kale has thirty times more vitamin C, especially the outer leaves. Raw spinach has six times the calcium, although its iron content is negligible compared to that of basil. And other types of lettuce, such as Simpson and Butterhead, have twice the potassium.

A salad is supposed to be a colorful toss of whatever is young and fresh in the vegetable department. Please, don't walk past herbs. Aside from emphatic flavor, they enrich your dish with nutrients that come in numbers like Alpine elevations. Basil has 10,000 units of vitamin A. Pinch nasturtium leaves; they are peppered with calcium and potassium. Roquette, my favorite, has 469 milligrams of calcium. Beet greens contain 647 milligrams of potassium. And you throw them out!? Parsley, served as a decoration in public eateries and mostly left on the plate, has 195 milligrams of vitamin C and enough chlorophyll to sweeten your breath.

Popeye gobbled spinach for that burst of energy he needed to save his true love, Olive Oyl, from her seducers. That scrawny string bean probably could have handled her own problems nicely if her diet had included plenty of that pure or virgin product she was named for: olive oil. Would it surprise you to learn that part of the reason for low cardiovascular fatality rates in some countries is, in fact, olive oil? It has been documented that the mortality rate in Greece and Crete is among the lowest. It's one of the areas where olive oil consumption is highest. Among men in Corfu, twenty or less per thousand die due to heart disease. Contrary to other cooking fats, it does not raise the level of cholesterol in the blood; it probably helps to lower it.

Olive oil has been part of cooking traditions since ancient times. Thousand-year-old trees are still productive in the Fertile Crescent, the cradle of Western civilization. Whether heated or unheated, it may reduce gastric acidity and may even be effective in protecting against ulcers and gastritis. Of all the oils, it's the one best absorbed by the intestines. It aids normal bone growth and permits improved bone mineralization in children and also in adults, which is certainly of interest to women. "It's also the most suitable fat for preventing the wear and tear of age on the functions of the brain, and on aging of tissues and organs in general."* If you are not familiar with its use, experiment with various flavors. You might find that, due to its viscosity and fruity taste, less of it is required, especially in a Teflon-coated frying pan—thus saving on calories. It's been around for eight thousand years.

How many times a day do we think about food? More often than we're willing to confess. There must be hundreds of thousands of ways to prepare the basic things we eat: meat, poultry, fish, fruit, vegetables, salad, starch, eggs, dairy, and sweets. Yet, I believe most of us limit ourselves to just a few variations in the dishes we choose. Heritage has a strong influence.

You can often recognize a person's national origin by how he eats. Not only what, but how. Americans juggle cutlery from hand to hand and, if well trained, will rest the knife across the top of the plate between bites. Some cut all or most of their food into morsels, like mother did when they were little. Small-fry in northern Europe have their own pusher. Who? No, what! It's a mini hoe that helps them load the spoon or fork. Typically continental is to eat slowly. A midday meal in a French bistro lasts several hours. There's wine and, of course, bread. Without bread, how could one finish what's on the plate? First, you need to tear small pieces to stick on the fork, so that all the gravy can be wiped up, bite by bite. Sauce, after all, is the pride of every French kitchen. Before dessert, there's always an array of regional cheeses, with more bread. Folks sit and rest, talk and linger. Restaurants don't seem to expect a second, third, or fourth seating.

And yet, how we eat isn't nearly as important as what we eat. More and more scientists believe that the modern diet isn't good for us. What we put on the plate is one problem. What Americans leave on the plate is another. Stems of broccoli: iron! Crusts of bread: fiber! Fat trimmed off steak: now there you're doing just fine! But we can't trim a greasy hamburger served on a totally useless roll. What else do we reject? Idaho potato skins with fabulous fiber. Parsley. Watercress. How did they get to be just decoration? We *drink* oranges, *peel* apples, core cabbage, and spit watermelon seeds as a contest. The worst offense we have perpetuated, in misguided affluence, is the bugaboo that to leave an empty plate is bad manners. Somewhere we got the mistaken notion that hostess, mother, or restaurateur might interpret this as a sign of not having served ample portions.

When choosing a town or neighborhood in which to settle, young families usually first investigate the quality of the schools. It's one way of judging the type of citizens who will be their neighbors and their children's companions. But don't overlook the nearby supermarket as a guidepost to the financial, ethnic, and social background of families in the area. The ever more elaborate take-out counters are crowded where working parents shop. They spend a large chunk of their income on freshly made provisions that have tall price tags: eight dollars a pound for shrimp salad; ready-made garden salad for five dollars; egg salad for four dollars; a six-ounce blister pack of salami and cheese for three dollars; clam chowder, serving one, for two dollars.

One view from the bridge was expressed by a garbage-scow captain who took Anita Loos and me for a ride around Manhattan when we were gathering material for our book *Twice Over Lightly*. He told us that he picks up the most garbage from the poorest neighborhoods and much less from affluent areas.

The famous chef Brillat-Savarin said: "Tell me what you eat and I will tell you what you are." If the baking-from-scratch products sell well in your market, I suppose there are more mothers at home than at work. If you notice many well-stocked shelves of ethnic foods of all kinds, no doubt the complexion of the neighborhood is very American, namely mixed. Ancestral, cultural, and geographic history is evident in the foods we prefer. Irish cuisine is basic and hearty. The French fuss a lot more. Russians can't make it without sour cream and beets; South Americans without pepper and cumin; Italians without pesto and pignolis; and Germans without potatoes. Wonderful new foods are more and more prevalent since Koreans and other Asians have joined our national portrait in greater numbers. They brought pungent, fresh ginger to our chopping board.

Sometimes local color can be too much for uninitiated

senses. I remember being served kimchi at a banquet in Korea, given by the President of Seoul University. I tried the best I could to hide from the aroma behind my napkin. This spicy cabbage concoction, prepared in covered earthen jars, is buried in the ground—for the whole winter. There was no escape from its redolence. No, make that its awful odor!

You need not peek in your neighbors' window. You can get a glimpse of their cultural beginnings by studying their market baskets.

* International Olive Oil Council. Contact Bette E. Gollrad. (212) 683-4900

The Elegant Body

Limousines have never been my favorite way to get from here to there. I much prefer to walk. On a recent trip to Washington, my gracious host provided me with one of those stretch limos with black windows. I felt as though I were being transported to my final resting place. Instead of being able to feast my eyes on my favorite city, I had to stare at the blank TV screen in front of me and watch liquor bounce around in crystal decanters.

I have walked with enthusiasm since my playpen days and, starting at the age of five or six, between rehearsals and performances of every play. When we were touring with a play, my fellow actors used to voluntarily share the hours when they were responsible for walking with me. I'm afraid the stage manager did not trust me to be back in time for the performance. I actually did get lost once in Lincoln Park, in Chicago—couldn't find my way out. I still walk, everyday, in every place I happen to be.

Walking is the best of all exercises for physical fitness and mental outlook. I consider it a form of life insurance. Unlike many other sports, it helps use the body *evenly*. Walking leisurely, at about a mile per hour, may not sound like much, but it is a good way to start when you plan to increase the distance and speed a little each day. If you eat your main meal in the evening, you should never miss that old-fashioned after-dinner walk; not just ten minutes with the dog, but an hour to buy the paper or a carton of milk. Walking to work, if at all possible, in many cases will not take much more time than waiting for transportation or being caught in traffic. Walking to business appointments within the city often saves time. Lunch hour presents an opportunity to test the theory that walking depresses the appetite. Instead of heading right for a restaurant, walk for thirty minutes. You will be much less hungry than you thought.

It takes conscious effort to withstand the conveniences that enable us to become fat and lazy. "A continuing study of nearly 17,000 Harvard alumni has demonstrated that moderate exercise in adult life can significantly increase life expectancy."* You realize, of course, that those are the same 17,000 bright minds that shower us with every conceivable labor-saving device currently known to man. They devote all their time and talent to making sure we need not walk, lift, climb, carry, dig, hammer, heave, bend, push, or pull. By now, we are almost unaware how many functions are performed for us without so much as a blink of an eyelid or the twitch of a muscle. "Men who participate in walking, stair climbing, and sports that use 2,000 calories or more a week had death rates one-fourth to one-third lower than those (in the study) who were least active.† I think perhaps the secret word, as Groucho used to say, is "the study." They may mean by that not their research project but the *study;* that cozy den where the green-eyed cyclops holds us in thrall, keeping us totally immobilized many hours every evening.

Just about everything runs by remote control. We need not get up from the chair to switch TV channels, lower the volume (who ever *lowers* the volume?), let out the dog, put on the kettle, dry the laundry, open the garage. The state-of-the-art house and office run themselves. Stay in bed and select favorite scenes from old movies, tape-record new ones, and zap the commercials. Voice command shuts the lights, raises the blinds, turns on the stove. Answer the phone without so much as turning your head or lifting your arm. Perfect the environment through thermostats programmed for cozy warmth and cool comfort. Unified master components transmit orders to a whole array of gadgets. We "talk" to them; they are capable of learning our language. A Swiss version, several steps ahead, can go around corners into the next room. I fear the phrase "broad-based" quite accurately describes the shape we'll all be in.

An amusing J. Seward Johnson sculpture portrays a life-size, lifelike businessman, with raincoat and briefcase, frantically hailing a cab from the door of the office tower. You know he is frantic because he is fifteen steps from the curb; and, although this executive replica seems young and strong, he wants his transportation within reach of his outstretched arm. Perhaps, he is the copywriter for this advertisement: "Electronic Motorized Treadmill for total control of your workout; with digital readout to monitor time, distance, and speed; enables running up to eight miles per hour at an incline of 15% grade. While running, speed is increased or decreased at the touch of a finger." All this for a mere $2,295! No wonder the poor man wants a taxi to come right up the sidewalk. He's exhausted!

We must have mechanical means to exercise our bodies because we have machines do everything else for us. You do not even have to squint or stoop to read the bathroom scale. A microprocessor-controlled scale will automatically announce your weight (in pounds and kilos) in a clear, digitally synthesized voice; it will also tell you how much you have lost or gained and will say: "Have a nice day" or "Goodbye" (whichever you'd prefer to have heard from your family). It will announce overload when 287 pounds are thrust upon it. In case this tempts you to drive off the edge of the world, you can precool or preheat your car with a remote-control car-starter. If traveling to exotic places is becoming too much of a hassle, consider The Antilles Environment Salon for the home. It uses heat and water to simulate any weather and season you choose and can be had for around $17,000, installation not included. Remember dumbbells?

B. F. Skinner, exponent of behaviorism, wants us to know about the negative consequences of too much of a good thing. Among other things, we are deprived of the strengthening consequences of labor. We strive for a life of ease but don't necessarily find happiness when we get there. We look at beautiful things, listen to wonderful music, attend the best theater, watch exciting entertainment and informational material, and eat delicious food. Yet Skinner paints a drastic portrait of the future. While we expend relatively little effort to get our share, we are unleashing forces that may destroy us: Nuclear power. Genetic engineering. Fossil fuel pollution. Unchecked population growth. New, harrowing pestilence. Power politics. Irreversible environmental destruction. The devastating possibilities are known to everyone. When will we change? Can it be done democratically?

Under the spur of Sputnik, we revved up science and math in every school. With John Kennedy's determination, physical fitness came out from under the basketball hoop onto the exercise mat. Brainy kids were no longer eggheads, and brawny kids were no longer ruffians. Now where are we? "American schoolchildren, in some cases, are significantly weaker than a decade ago. In areas such as running, jumping, flexibility, and strength, the statistics are alarming."‡ (What do you mean we're not a sports-conscious nation! Over 100 million people sit and watch the Super Bowl!) Forty percent of boys six to twelve and seventy percent of girls cannot do more than one pull-up on a raised bar. More than half of the girls could not do even one. Nor could these children reach beyond their toes while seated on the floor with their legs outstretched. Lack of fitness in youth could lead to so many problems, I hate to even think about it.

It wouldn't surprise me if the most frequently bought gifts and gift certificates are sport and exercise related. How does Santa get Nautilus equipment and exercycles down chimneys? He must be in better shape than he appears to be. Gifts like these show we know what's good for everyone; they are an affirmation of how much we love them, an admonition to take better care of themselves. (Of course, we also present untold gallons of liquor, but that's a whole other matter.) You didn't forget to brush your teeth this morning, right? It's habitual and doesn't call for a decision. So, why is it necessary to make a conscious effort, every day, to take the time to exercise? Roll out of bed into a robe, stagger to the kitchen for a cup of coffee; from there, to the shower and into street clothes, and off you go, still with the internal system at rest, into an environment switched to high gear.

Getting up twenty minutes earlier sounds cruel to hard-working people. But once they find out that ritual exercise energizes them for the whole day, they are less inclined to skip it. It takes discipline to make it a priority. It is a mistake to set goals that may be unattainable. Don't expect to lose weight; you may be just redistributing it—new muscles, less flab. You will be less nervous, less tired, and less irritable. Your outlook on life will improve, if for no other reason than that you are pleased with yourself. Merely keeping an appointment with yourself is gratifying. Attend at least one exercise class a week. Fresh ideas and variety are important to help you stick to it. If all else fails, find a friend who will join you in mutual self-motivation; it will obligate both of you to keep at it.

"Exercise" is no longer the worst word in the American lexicon. We have finally caught on to it; in every other corner of the globe it had always been quite acceptable. The Chinese do calisthenics in the street, in unison. The Russians do it in factories and offices, in place of a coffee break. Northern Europeans probably invented it, and schools have always forced it on scholars. Currently, dinner conversations are a toss-up between miles covered with the "greatest, sixty-dollar running shoes" and inches lost on a "fabulous fad diet". Yet if you decide to do a few surreptitious stretches during a transatlantic flight, stiffly strapped seatmates think you are just a bit weird. I suggest, at the risk of sounding too communal, that airlines design a ten-minute exercise program, projected on the screen, to encourage passengers to participate in unkinking.

Many limbering muscle stretches and oxygenating exercises are appropriate for in-flight conditioning. The strain of having sat, motionless, for too long can ruin the first days of a vacation. Long hours of inactivity decrease the oxygen in our veins. One should not have to pretend to be looking for something on the floor or in the overhead rack just to get a good stretch of the spine. A well-thought-out set of stretches, bends, and pulls, illustrated on the screen, will limber up a whole planeload of passengers. They will be a lot less cranky and restless and will have fun in the process. Yoga breathing exercises lift the mood and energize everyone aboard. The session could end with humming a mantra, in unison. Now, don't laugh. Aren't all those clones, sitting and staring into space with rented listening devices clamped to their heads, willingly participating in preprogrammed sound?

* *The New England Journal of Medicine*, March 6, 1986, Vol. 314 #10
† Ibid.
‡ The President's Council on Physical Fitness and Sports

You're in Charge!

"Maybe you should go to see your doctor." What else can one think to say when friends and relatives enumerate their aches and pains? We are accustomed to specialization. To rely on our own judgment, experience, knowledge, common sense, well, that's pretty cheeky, isn't it? There is so much information coming at us, every day, about health and medicine that we believe (*a*) we should never get sick, and (*b*) if we do, there *is* a cure. Does a common cold have to run its course? Of course. Does a back pain lead to permanent disability? Not if some sensible changes are incorporated into one's daily routine. "Our real goal (in research), is the improvement of human health; medical progress is, by far, the least important factor in human health. The two most important factors are life-style and environment. We believe in research to find a cure for every known ill. But prevention, on which no time and money is spent, would save so many more people. For every person saved by something resulting from research, we lose an unaccountably greater number of people."*

In Martin Walser's novel *The Inner Man*, you find this unusual advice from a physician to his patient: "Self-help is more important than any medication. Your metabolism depends on mental effort. To whom do you think that complicated metabolic system is listening? To you! You call the tune. And, if you produce only discordant notes, you mustn't be surprised at the discordant notes with which your physical apparatus answers you. You seem to take particular pleasure in letting your body suffer at your own hands. To whom do you want to display this suffering? We are always out to impress somebody. That's the strongest of all motives." If this were framed and hanging on the wall, doctors' waiting rooms would be less crowded.

"Fat blood can be a real heartbreaker." According to the American Heart Association, about half the adults over forty in this country have this condition. Eating out is part of the problem. Fine restaurants still pride themselves on cream sauces, egg custards, butter broiling, cheese richness, milk-fed veal—up, up into a fluffy gourmet heaven. The food industry is only just now becoming aware that consumers need a little help in changing their eating habits. Fast-food restaurants are a long way from making it easy to avoid dipped-in-egg batter, barbecued ribs, all-you-can-eat specials, fatty beef patties, and the oldest of standbys, eggs 'n' bacon. Uncontested culprits are cream substitutes made from coconut oil. "In 1973, Americans consumed 42% of their calories from fat." Have we gotten smarter? Ten years later, the figure was forty-three percent, though now we consume less butter, eggs, and whole milk.

Health is as big a subject as love, sports, and success. At home, we can adjust our menus and substitute ingredients in recipes: egg whites instead of whole eggs; skim milk in place of whole milk products; vegetables cooked in vermouth and lemon instead of butter; ground turkey in place of ground beef; corn oil, not vegetable oil; Parmesan cheese for mozzarella; egg whites in a mousse in place of heavy cream; chicken instead of shrimp. Has anyone published a concise guide for substituting ingredients? It seems a logical project. Then those of us who like to cook will see that a portion of lasagna can be twenty-five milligrams lower in cholesterol if we use vegetables instead of beef, low-fat cottage cheese, and skim-milk mozzarella. What we eat can save more medical dollars than fastened seat belts.

The Center for Science in the Public Interest, a consumer research organization, reports on how food is prepared in eight of the largest fast-food chains in the country. You may be as shocked as most people to learn that our favorite eateries prepare french fries in beef drippings, lard, and other fats that are highly saturated. As we all know by now, these fats contribute to heart disease. Some fast-food chains use palm oil, which is even more unhealthy, although it disguises its shortcomings as a shortening by being called a vegetable oil. "Many parents are unwittingly exposing their children to the increased likelihood of heart disease by allowing them to eat at fast-food outlets. It would be safer to tell them 'go out and play in traffic.' "† Food chains say they cater to our tastes. That is so, no doubt. But tastes are acquired. If it is a "treat" to be taken out for a Coke, burger, and fries, then that is what we learn to love, however it is prepared. If it had always been cider, lean ham, and baked beans instead, then that would be every kid's favorite. "Many restaurants use the same shortening to fry and bake most foods—pies, chicken nuggets, fish, and others." Dr. William Castelli directs a medical inquiry that has been going on for thirty-six years. He says that "fat in the diet is clearly a major cause of heart disease. We have to get it out of our diet." At your favorite counter, ask what's bubbling in their cauldron. And don't accept a vague answer about "highest quality or a blend." You don't want ninety percent animal fat and ten percent vegetable oil.

The U. S. Public Health Service speculates that life expectancy may easily increase sixteen years when all degenerative diseases have been eliminated. What do we have to do to reach that projected goal of ninety-plus years? Put the mind in charge of body and brain! Sounds simple, but where to start? More important, when to start? Now. Fifty or fifteen, thirty-five or eighty-five, it is not too soon *and never too late* to make use of three tools at our disposal: nutrition, exercise, stress management. Suppose the local TV network were to do a segment of the evening news on you, would you be an inspiration for your age group? *Not* if you stayed in bed till it was time to grab a cup of coffee and dash for the train. *Not* if you had two sunny-side-ups and sausages, white toast, jam, and butter for breakfast. Not if a Big Mac is your favorite lunch and chops are the dinner menu of choice.

Degenerative disease is not entirely avoidable, but we can hasten or halt it by sheer willpower. The average American diet is excessively high in fat, animal protein, and refined carbohydrates. Exercise is the best method for transporting the resulting cholesterol through the bloodstream. Exercise, not now and then, not two weeks in the summer, not Sunday golf, but a ten-to fifteen-minute morning *routine* and a brisk walk at least once a day to minimize the damage we do by what we eat and our sedentary life.

We are, by nature, engineered to react with our whole system to fear, anger, and hostility. But modern life has taken us out of the paths of lions, crocodiles, and volcanoes. Instead, we dramatize our existence with uncalled-for stress, which should and can be managed. We should realize how inconsequential most of it is and learn to become more flexible. Stress triggers the majority of heart attacks.

Most of us have our own way of handling tension and anxiety. The man who slams out of the house and goes for a long walk to avoid arguments happens to be doing the right thing. So does the woman who decides this is the moment to take down the curtains and wash the windows. The youngster who escapes from school or parental pressure by batting a ball against the house for an hour is tranquilizing his mental agitation without drugs. Valium and other drugs of that type used to be prescribed like aspirin, with total disregard for possible side effects and withdrawal symptoms. It is not safe and risk-free as it was once thought to be. Patients who attempt gradual withdrawal from Valium, even under medical supervision, often develop extreme distress.

There is great concern about the risk of addiction to Valium and similar drugs. Withdrawal symptoms include tremors, dizziness, insomnia, and other discomforts. If you are saying to yourselves that this does not concern you, you only "take a little" only "now and then," then who is consuming four billion doses of prescription tranquilizers at a cost of $2 billion a year? The best prescription against anxiety and tension is always available at a price you can't beat. An energetic hike, scrubbing the floor, throwing a bowling ball, mowing a lawn, is as effective as any tranquilizing drug with only beneficial side effects. You can't run out of it, no one can use it up before you get your hands on it. You don't have to hide it or hoard it. It can't kill you or cause mental aberrations. And yes, you will become addicted. But you won't crash.

Try to open a jar that's stuck or tighten a bolt that's resisting your efforts, and the strain will probably cause you to clench your molars. Intense effort can make us bite down so hard that it causes pain. Physical stress can put strain on the jaw. So can mental stress. You might think you can train yourself to prevent it. But people who unconsciously clench or gnash their teeth and tighten their mouth muscles do it also in their sleep. Wake up with an ear ache, and you suspect infection. If it is a headache, you wonder if a virus has invaded or your sinuses are acting up. If your teeth hurt, you calculate back to the last dental visit and chide yourself. Ringing ears, back pain, or neck stiffness, and there you have it!—old age is creeping up on you. But, those can all be symptoms of tension, physical or mental. It afflicts as many as twenty-four percent of us. And, I suspect, a lot of medicine is dispensed by unsuspecting doctors for these symptoms without an ailment.

Jaw clenching causes many painful conditions, which will only get worse unless either the tension or the clenching is prevented. If your jaw feels tired when you wake up in the morning, see your dentist, not your pharmacist. You may need to have a bite plate fashioned for you that will prevent your back teeth from touching while you sleep. It is worn only at night. "The TMJ Syndrome (as it's called), hinges on a U-shaped piece of cartilage that forms a cushion between the jaw bone and the skull."‡ When it is stretched abnormally, it can slip, producing a clicking, popping, or rubbing sound. And sharp pain. Pain, as we know, can radiate to other parts of the body, making it hard to associate it with its source. Watch the late news before you hit the pillow and don't be too surprised if, in the morning, you feel as if it's been hitting back. Until the 1970s, not much was known about these tension-produced discomforts. We have become more informed about medicine (and too informed about the madness loose in the world).

I am a reader of advertisements. The prose is often more skillful than most writing and more succinct because of the high cost per line, per page. I admire attention-getters, subtle or blunt. I loved the caption that assumes my skin is living too fast. They don't ask! They know! The lost hours of sleep. The skipped meals. The pace. The product is touted as the ultimate survival plan for complexions. Another ad not to be overlooked asks: "Are your teeth older than you are?" Anthropologists have found human teeth, millions of years old, which have survived just about everything nature could throw at them. Of course, that was before white bread, ground steak, and cooked carrots. It is quite true that "once the teeth age prematurely, the likelihood is that the rest of the body is not far behind." A quote from Dr. Mayo (of the famous clinic) points out the "definite connection between bodily health and oral health: Preventive dentistry can extend human life ten years." To accomplish this, we must spend a lot of time caring for teeth *and* gums—not just ten seconds, twice a day—but ten minutes! Your dentist can teach you how to do it, but only *you* can save your teeth, unless you see *him* twice a day.

Medical quackery costs millions of dollars each year. A variety of ineffective, expensive, and sometimes harmful devices, products, and treatments are said to provide miraculous health "cures." Some products and services pose little or no health risk, but they do swindle you out of your money. These so-called cures generally can be classified into two groups: quack products and quack services. Some of the products can actually harm you, even when used as directed. The services can hurt you indirectly because their use delays your seeking proper medical diagnosis and care. Medical scientists generally agree that you cannot lose weight, for any length of time, without diet and/or exercise. Pills, preparations, body wraps, vibrating machines, and food supplements with dieting are, at best, unproven. No over-the-counter or through-the-mail pill, cream, bath, or wrap can contour, enlarge, or reduce inches from selected parts of the body. It is impossible to grow new hair by using massages and creams. Synthetic hair implants are illegal and have been known to cause serious infections. Electrolysis, when performed by a physician, is an effective way of removing hair, but do-it-yourself methods are usually ineffective and painful. Copper or other metal bracelets, unproven or banned drugs, bath treatments, and fancy-looking machines cannot cure or prevent arthritis. No device or product can reverse or prevent the aging process. If you realize you have purchased a quack device or product, report it to your physician or, perhaps, the Better Business Bureau, county medical society, local or state health department, local or state consumer affairs office, or state attorney general. What keeps so many of these carnival con artists in business is our sheepish embarrassment, which prevents us from complaining.

The best medical news in recent months has been on cancer research. No news whatsoever on head colds. That's not surprising, if you realize there are more than a hundred different viruses that can cause a cold. The sheer numbers make it impossible to develop a vaccine to protect us from all of them. A bulletin from a nationwide drug chain confirms what I have always believed: "Nothing will cure or shorten a cold, including vitamin C or antibiotics." (Antibiotics treat bacterial infections, not viruses!) I admire such honesty, since Americans run to the drugstore with $500 to $700 million a year to treat their colds, coughs, and allergies. So, on just one annual cold, which will run its course in five to seven days, we spend $100 million *a day!* Unfortunately, one cold won't make us immune to a second one. If you are not careful about washing your hands frequently, you could reinfect yourself.

Contrary to what your mother may have drummed into your head, colds are not caused by chilling, wet feet, or running off without your hat. And, contrary to what current wisdom denies, you *can* catch it from a doorknob. Yes, and from shaking hands. Even a table, where a used tissue has rested, can spread contagion. Some viruses can live for several days on a hard surface. Fine droplets of moisture on the breath of a cold sufferer who coughs, sneezes, or speaks will spread a cold. We are most contagious during the one to four days of incubation, *before* symptoms are apparent. It remains true that fatigue, tension, or poor diet will make us more prone to catching a cold. So perhaps tired, cold, wet feet play a part, after all. Germicidal facial tissues especially treated to reduce the life span of viruses (still in the experimental phase) promise that soon we'll be able to toss out the common cold.

* Steven Tiger, physician assistant and guest lecturer in medical physiology in Brooklyn Hospital-Long Island University Physician Assistant Program
† Dr. Tazewell Banks, Professor of Medicine at D. C. General Hospital
‡ *USA Today*, February 1985

Spirits on Wheels

The agonies of alcoholism have been familiar to me since early childhood. Childhood is rather brief under those conditions. I soon became my mother's mother and she the child. I have been witness to it in all its aspects—its destruction, its charm and delight. There was Jack Barrymore, so amusing, so witty. The bottle sharpened his understanding and increased his sensitivity to the performance. But it got out of hand, as it always will. I spent a whole season with Richard Burton in *Time Remembered*, suffering the tortures. Knowing my feelings about drink, he amused himself with my distress. When we bowed low, hand in hand, at the end of each performance, he would whisper, "I had two tonight." That meant he had consumed two fifths of vodka in his dressing room, with the help of some friends who kept dropping in because he was a beguiling and entertaining man. He delighted in taunting me, bragging, making an impression. My admiration for him, and my recommendation that he be my costar, were not enough. He had to get closer, more personal; and that was his way, by laughing.

"We can only be as healthy as our customers." I like that slogan. It fits so many product categories: cars, frankfurters,

TV programs, tobacco. It comes from the Distilled Spirits
Council, trade association of the liquor industry. The pro-
ducers of intoxicating beverages are concerned over the
misuse of alcohol and are developing a sense of responsibility. Bacardi rum has an admonition right on the label: "Enjoy It, In Moderation." A mild caution is better than none.
An industry that spends an estimated $1.2 billion to pro-
mote its products should shoulder some of the responsibility for educating the ultimate user. Others around the country are also getting into the act.

There is a ground swell of public action against drunken
driving. Organized groups work to change and enforce
stricter laws. Bartenders can now be sued for serving inebriated patrons. Citizens band radios were all the rage a few
years ago; I wonder why they fell on hard times so soon.
Overconsumption, perhaps. Yet, if every car were to be
equipped, by the manufacturer, with a means to contact the
highway patrol, wouldn't drunkenness behind the wheel
diminish? "Truckers Against Drunk Drivers" help to warn
others on the road and alert police to inebriated drivers
they notice weaving, speeding, or nodding off. Half of road
fatalities are alcohol-related—23,500 drunk-driving deaths
a year. Surgeons also have a group that lobbies for stricter
laws to fight drunkenness. After all, they're the ones who
must sew up the wrecked bodies, if they can. The State of
Maine has an educational program called "Project Graduation" because so many young people never made it past the
Senior Night beer bash. The first year of this campaign,
every senior managed to show up—in cap and gown—to
accept the diploma in person.

For in-depth knowledge of alcoholism you may want to
tackle *The Natural History of Alcoholism,* by Professor George
Vaillant. In its 359 pages, you will find a very well documented, forty-year-long study of six hundred men. Having
plowed through all the research, one arrives at the conclusion that Alcoholics Anonymous seems to have been on the
right track all along. Recovery apparently depends on discovering a substitute dependency. Members of AA, or a

similar social support group, are usually totally dedicated. The peer-group meetings are a source of inspiration, hope, and can renew battered self-esteem. Professor Vaillant points out that it is not personality disorders that bring on alcoholism. Depression and loss of control over one's life are not the causes but the results. Heredity and ethnic background, as well as personal antisocial behavior, increase the risk of alcohol dependency. Fetal alcoholism is sometimes the source of lifelong addiction. Childhood trauma is less likely to be a cause if the parents were not alcoholics. Yet even the most stable family situations are no guarantee against addiction if the parent is an alcoholic.

Little progress has been made in the last twenty-five years in combatting this dangerous personal and public disease. The ultimate cure is always, and only, in the hands of the patients, who must treat themselves. Dr. Vaillant writes: "Staying sober is not a process of simply becoming detoxified, but often becomes the work of several years, even a lifetime."

The private sector is getting involved. *Reader's Digest* is living up to its advertising slogan: "We make a difference." Together with the Board of Directors of The One Club for Art and Copy in New York, they sponsored a poster contest against teenage drunk driving—to stop high-school students from killing themselves by driving drunk or riding in cars with drunk drivers. A challenge was issued to high school students across the land to devise programs against drunk driving. Students then put their programs into effect and sent in documented results to show how well they worked. At commencement time, the Reader's Digest Foundation awarded $500,000 in four-year college scholarships to the students who devised the best programs. The second part of the challenge was directed to the creative minds and artistic hands in advertising agencies. They were asked to design posters to be sent to nearly every high school. The art director and copywriter who created the best poster each won a week for two in Paris.

An article written by a grief-stricken father whose son was

killed by a drunk driver prompted this competition. I think
you might be interested in the results. I hope I can describe
them well enough; they all have exceedingly powerful visu-
als. In first place: a handsome portrait of smiling Stevie
Wonder, behind his inscrutable sunglasses. The message is
unmistakable: "Before I'll ride with a drunk, I'll drive myself!" Second place was awarded to a five-foot-long poster:
"Last year, 7,514 high school students stopped drinking
and driving." A stark charcoal drawing illustrates the point
—a body bag shrouding a corpse strapped, tagged, ready
for removal. The third-prize winners designed a masterful
graphic in black and white: a double row of gleaming steel
doors in an otherwise bare city morgue. The legend beneath this photo comes straight to the point. "There are no
heroes in this locker room." If there is one thing a teenager
prizes, it is his car, be it a low-slung red "Vette" or an old
heap bandaged with lavish love. A creative advertising team
from Boston won only eighth place, but their plea not to
drive drunk outranks even vintage Volkswagen ads. Picture
this: "Last night, Jimmy Dennehy traded his Chevy for a
Cadillac." Below, on black background, shines a long black
limousine, curtained side window, a boxy back end. It is a
hearse.

What can you do to stop drunk driving? Many suggestions are made. Not enough are acted upon. Yes, you can
call the police to report the car you see careening down the
highway. But by the time you get to the phone, the car that's
endangering others may well be out of the jurisdiction of
the station you called. It carries with it the danger of a
police-state mentality, where citizens are expected to report
each other's illegal behavior. If you see a drunk leave a bar
heading for the car, it is suggested you tell the bartender to
detain him or her. "Dramshop" laws in many states make
bars, restaurants, and liquor shops liable for damage caused
by a drunk driver they have served. I can't imagine an inn-
keeper will listen to a stranger off the street telling him how
to handle his clientele. One of the most effective ways to

stem the tide of drunk driving is to vote for tougher judges
and lobby for stricter enforcement of laws.

In New Philadelphia, Ohio, it was the wisdom of a municipal judge that decreased the liquor-induced carnage on the
roads of Tuscarawas County. Edward O'Farrell sentenced
every first-time offender to fifteen days in jail, a $750 fine,
and a six-month driver's license suspension. He said "most
judges would get tougher on drunk drivers if people in their
communities let them know that they are unhappy about
leniency." He suggests that citizens ask local news media to
publicize the sentencing records of judges. Then, if lenient
judges don't get tough on drunk drivers, the constituency
must campaign against them.

Carriage Trade

Kids are tough. Newborn babies managed to survive the Mexican earthquake, buried for days in the rubble of a hospital. Nature provided them with a number of extraordinary means for survival. And who knows, supernatural forces might have been at work, as well!

Parents, too, have extraordinary power and influence. Having children is for the young. That is the eternal plan. But, it has been tampered with, to some extent. Having them a bit later, or a lot later, is quite common now. When marriages took place as a matter of course in one's late teens, offspring followed soon after. "Well, are you pregnant yet?" is what mothers-in-law could not resist asking. And sooner, in preference to later, most couples obliged dutifully. Did they have clearer reasons then for having children? Perhaps not. Fewer options, yes. The specter of divorce and the pressure of twin careers were less prevalent.

Compromises necessary to raise a family have not changed. Money. Time. Personal freedom. Job requirements. Living space. Inconvenience. Disruption. Self-denial. Interference. Obligation. The list of possible, no probable, problems and deprivations is endless. The anguish of couples in their thirties trying to decide yea or nay on child rearing is pitiful to contemplate. Does one have to be totally selfless to have a child? Perhaps what is needed are truly selfish reasons. The act of creation is far too compelling. We have a need to give love, to teach, to influence character, to share our life, to perpetuate ourselves. It *is* right to feel selfish about a child, without whom one may feel incomplete. To have one because it is the eleventh hour, because it is fashionable again, or because parents are eager for a grandchild are not good enough reasons. If life is already fraught with problem-solving, don't add children into the mix.

The news in population growth is the "baby boomlet." Just what affects these cycles is hard to say. Many things influence us to expand or minimize personal responsibilities. Astute architects are incorporating more flexibility into their plans. Schools, when not needed, are turned into senior centers or office buildings and back again. Private homes, too, must have built-in possibilities. First, for only two people, then to include children; later, as shared accommodation, perhaps with aging relatives, and back again.

Have you noticed, as I have, the absence of afternoon and weekend "child sounds" in your neighborhood? Though there are more children now than a few years ago, where are they? Playing hide-and-seek? No, hiding! Hiding from reality! One way to do that is to watch a lot of television, which very quickly makes everything unreal to the young mind. Children are also being hidden by their alarmed parents.I don't mean they are prisoners. They are being sequestered in school, day care, after-school programs, preschool, baby co-ops, play groups. They are not allowed to play on the sidewalk, in the backyard, or at neighbors'. The carriage trade is deprived of the sandbox and the company of other children, unless it is on an organized basis. Working mothers take *after-dinner* walks together, pushing carriages in the night air! The latest in board games for the older children (are you ready for this?), Strangers & Dangers, Don't Talk to Strangers, and Safely Home. These games, which are meant to help combat child abuse and abduction, push the onus for a secure childhood on our *children*. Do you remember Jules Feiffer's *Little Murders*, the play and motion picture? I recommend you reread it, if you want to know in which direction we are headed.

Childhood is a short season. Sometimes, its time span is artificially manipulated. At the moment, child rearing is swinging in the direction of self-conscious overemphasis. Mothers have always had conversations with in utero beings. This communication has some validity. Now, I'm afraid, they think they are already *teaching* the fetus. How sad. Teaching can wait. Infancy is a time for unstructured enjoyment. The six-month-old who learns to swim may be made safer in a disaster at sea. But he is also being made an example of parental competence. Flash cards for math, music, and foreign language from birth! Whatever for? Just exactly what is the point of teaching reading before the first birthday? I have known children who could read the daily paper at three. If they understood what they were reading and retained it all, they may well be the ones who swell the teenage suicide statistics to the present, heartbreaking numbers.

Parents today raise their children by the book. They spend a lot of time organizing their time, and a lot of thought on how to cram maximum learning and experience into little heads. The mere thought exhausts me. It is wonderful that they are so involved with the upbringing and education of their children. But they should guard against blurring the boundary between childhood and maturity.

Of course this system prevailed already in the days when I had Mary. I remember going to dear Dr. Schloss, who was considered one of the finest pediatricians of his day in New York. He had all the "great" babies in his care from Pontico Hill to Gramercy Park. In my state of inexperience and insecurity I went to him to ask for guidance in devising a routine for my baby. And he said: "Oh, good grief, are you going to start organizing this child's life? Just leave her to have lots of private, quiet time, time to just develop into what she will be."

My own childhood was blessed by a mother who just wasn't "into parenting," as the phrase would go today. She neither lived her child's life for her nor her own life through me. In the days of Dr. Spock she would have been considered too casual, perhaps extremely neglectful. She was always involved with friends and bridge—with anything but that small child. She just couldn't be bothered. I think she didn't really want a child. Her interest in me didn't develop until I was beginning to be of some use in getting her out of the rut of housework.

My German godmother, Annie Hess, saw to my infant needs. I certainly remember this darling maiden lady with joy and fondness. My mother was off and running most of the time. So I had this marvelous *private* childhood. I made up my own amusements. My playmates and I did wonderfully inventive and creative things. We made clothes for penny-dolls from scraps of fabric. We made presents for each other and our parents. We invented life. I had imaginary playmates too. "The people in the wall" were a nonexistent family who lived in the "apartment house" in the wall next to my bed. They may well have been the genesis of my love for theater, for I scripted their comings and goings night after night before falling asleep.

We are in a state of overcommunication, where all knowledge and information is available to children. Toys are becoming so complicated that elders must first read instruction manuals, which tell them what age group each toy is for and what skills it will help to develop: "hand-eye coordination," "lesson in cause and effect," and suggestions on how to "stimulate the baby" (once called "peek-a-boo"). Pardon me if I am laughing just a little. Do college-bred Yuppies really need researchers to tell them how to play with their babies?

"What do you want to be when you grow up?" That old standby for creating rapport with a child does not work too well anymore. It can be too early for such a question: the future profession may not yet have been invented. If there is no immediate, definitive response, we may fall into the trap of suggesting a career and come off sounding sexist. Airline pilot for boys; secretary for girls; or other, frowned-upon stereotypes. There was a time when little boys would want to become soldiers after seeing a parade, or firemen when the engines clanged by. Daring, dangerous, masculine. Their sisters opted for nursing and practiced wearing caps. Subservient, care-giving, feminine. Now, they watch television and they know the truth. Soldiers get killed and police get into trouble. Doctors get sued and nurses are Amazons or sex objects. Entertainers get involved with drugs and legislators go afoul of the law. Tycoons are ruthless. Teachers are underpaid. Motherhood and household management are ignored, minimized, or deprecated. One beautiful exception—"The Bill Cosby Show," a happy picture of good parenthood.

It must be mighty difficult for children to fantasize about their future occupations. What heroic role models are there for boys and girls? What noble images can come to their minds? TV viewing is the most popular activity in the American family. It heads the list of preferred leisure-time occupation. Obviously, this is concentrated during prime time, when the family is together. Thus, the primary role models sit, staring at a box!

Growing Up
Is Hard to Do

Tom Stoppard's play *The Real Thing* does not state facts but poses an unanswerable question. What is Real? Whose Reality? One's perception depends on one's vantage point. I remember a Japanese film that explores that very theme— *Rashomon*, a story in which each character experiences the same event completely differently.

Television renders us almost immune to reality. The average American is said to watch seven hours a day, but admits to . . . you know . . . just the educational programs. Some will confess to using it for anesthesia, occupying the eye but withholding all thought while reality is flashed on the screen, often so painfully real that it hurts. ("20/20" saw value in broadcasting the stoning to death of a Haitian man —in all its bloody gore.) Cable TV tries to soothe us by bringing nature into the home. A "Mood Channel" based in Los Angeles televises hours of relentless ocean surf. If that is not the mood you're after, you can watch a fireplace, crackling and hissing with an occasional startling pop of collapsing logs. Hurry the day with a calming sunset or quicken the enervated pulse with a spectacular sunrise— complete with sounds of chirping birds awakening in their nests. For total withdrawal, silence, or catatonia, fish can be observed, mindlessly swimming around in an aquarium, for as long as you can stand it. But, for the mind in extreme agitation, there is "Walk-A-Shrink," a wonderful takeoff on a psychiatric session—forty-five minutes of taped "Hem . . . Ahum . . . Yeees? . . . How did that make you feel? . . . Go on . . . Why do think that is?" For six dollars, you can provide your own analytic responses during the long stretches of silence, which is just what you do for sixty dollars, anyhow.

More than twenty years ago, Laura Huxley wrote a book about the bewildering changes and uncertainties that confront us every day. The most outstanding element of her book is its title: *You Are Not the Target.* In those five words, we are given a maxim that can serve us well for a lifetime. Is a surly greeting a signal of rejection? Of course not. Should that cutting remark be taken personally? Probably not. The speaker usually suffers more than the one spoken to. Instead of dwelling on the unpleasantness one trips over each day, how much less affected we could be if only we remembered to say "I am not the target." Discomfort through words and actions by others is felt unnecessarily deeply, primarily because we are unsure of our own worth and importance. Laura Huxley (wife of Aldous Huxley, by the way) wished to influence us to create a chain reaction to improve the delicate balance between destructive and creative forces. We can "tip the balance in favor of intelligence, beauty, and love."

In order to realign our personal relationships, we can learn to deal with people who make us nervous, those who try to control us, those we fear, and others whom we only suspect of not liking us. But, of course, we must also modify *our* attitudes, which flow in the other direction and cause the same anguish to people we irritate, control, upset, and dislike. Here are a few of what Laura Huxley calls recipes: We each have the power to make ourselves and others feel better, or worse. Making others feel good is much more rewarding than making them feel bad. And perhaps most important, making others feel better generally makes us feel better too.

I was complaining to my friend and neighbor Margaret Davidson about my deteriorating memory. But she scolded me for taking so negative an attitude. She told me about her bouts with negative feelings when she was an editor at *Ladies' Home Journal*. Knowing that this was not the way to go about handling the pressures of deadlines, the responsibilities and the vagaries of creative people, she physically trained herself to lift the corners of her mouth. Whatever the crisis, she greeted it with those corners of her mouth raised just enough to make a positive impression, no matter how she felt inside. People would smile back, which always relieved tension and diffused potential confrontations. This woman instinctively understands that to be happy one must make others feel happy.

Self-respect is not a given; it must be acquired. We show our self-doubts in words and motions. "Body language" expresses a great deal about the inner self. Push the bangs back, one thousand times a day. Look over the heads of people we talk to. Lick the lips, pull the earlobe; an endless variety of insecurity. Words and phrases that pepper the language indicate a lack of confidence. "You know . . ." again and again in each sentence. "So I said . . ." "I hear ya . . ." "I know where you're coming from . . ."

What do you bring to the breakfast table? No, this is not a sermon on the cholesterol devils—eggs and bacon. Daytime rhythm is the subject. Everyone lives in a different time zone, so to speak. Some people can't utter a civil word before 11 A.M. Others seem to have swallowed a long-playing cassette while sleeping. And, with that first cup of coffee, we have an impasse between two people that beggars the Berlin Wall. One retreats behind a morning sulk or the morning paper; the other wants to tell every dream, make plans for every minute of the day, and replay yesterday in tight close-up. There is not much point in forcing the issue. The one who prefers to remain in the shell can't be coaxed, insulted, or shaken out of it. The talkative one had better find a method of storing the chatter for later, when the silent partner will be more amenable to conversation.

Hyper types start their days with an almost unbearable rush of energy and activity. Others must idle their motors for half a morning. If you are the "morning person" and live with one who is a slow starter, make appropriate allowances. Don't breakfast together. There is no need to sit glumly across from a newspaper, from behind which are broadcast not even a few spicy gossip items. To avoid the sullenness of silence, mention only subjects that are of interest to the quiet one, in such a way that a "yes" or "no" won't do.

Once we were children. We grow up. But should we? asks Ashley Montagu, anthropologist, anatomist, and lecturer. "Adults are deteriorated children," he says. All we really have done since infancy is increase in size, but not in form or shape. "We are designed to retain infantlike traits all our lives." The need for love, sensitivity, wonder, creativity, learning, exploration, and spontaneity are all part of our genetic constitution. As we go through stages of life, we undergo training designed to outgrow all this. "We have a social 'self' imposed on us early, and we wear it uncomfortably all our lives. We don't outgrow the needs we had as infants, but are taught to behave as if we have. These needs then remain unfulfilled." How many of our psychological pains and quirks lie in the fact that the childish qualities have been suppressed?

Montagu believes that "we have to understand aging as a process of growing and developing, not deteriorating. If we relearn to love, we will grow younger." Love is "communication, by demonstrative acts to others, of our concern and caring; that we will be there in case of need." Anyone can learn to become a loving person, at any age. All we have to do is act as if we are, long enough until it becomes comfortable and automatic. It *is* natural to us. We don't have to

learn it so much as to recall it. "Loving is one of our basic
developmental needs. It is always there for us to recapture."
The hostility and aggression we see in the world is a result
of childhood repression of the need for love. Men have had
their need for love more repressed than women. At the
annual meeting of health care and social service professionals of the American Society on Aging, there was an audible
gasp in the audience when Montagu claimed that "the most
dangerous creature on this earth is the white man."

Years of school attendance may serve to postpone adulthood. It may be wiser to go out into the world, the real
world, and "find yourself!" One might also encourage our
fine youth to go out and find the money to pay for their
education first. Four years of study costs in excess of
$20,000 in state colleges and up to $70,000 in private uni-
versities. According to some experts, many college students
are really not mature enough to benefit from their course of
study. "The reasons are not difficult to discover. As life
expectancy of Americans has increased, so has preparation
for adulthood. In a society that is taking longer to grow old,
the young are taking longer to grow up. Eighteen-year-olds
experience problems of independence, motivation, and social adaptation once encountered at an earlier age."* We
should not "blame adolescents for not being adults. To
become adults, the young need to be around adults."*
Mothers are out, working (probably to help pay for college).
Fathers are working overtime. Where are the grandparents?
In Florida? "In a society that is profoundly segregated by
age, an 'isolated youth culture' now fills the gap between
puberty and postponed adulthood."*

Instant gratification is part of this pleasure-seeking culture. It is not an idle recommendation that parents need
boldness to refuse to send their offspring to college—just
because they've reached their eighteenth birthday. Whether
mandatory public service or military conscription should
precede college, to allow for maturing, is debatable. The
Peace Corps and volunteering are other alternatives to six-

teen-plus years of uninterrupted schooling. Real jobs for our bright, hopeful, *inexperienced* youth are an even better idea. Working for a few years would lead to a more realistic view—of life and of themselves.

* *Grandparents/Grandchildren: The Vital Connection,* Woodward and Kornaber, Transaction Books, Rutgers University, New Brunswick, N.J., 1984

Love Affair
Between Hard Covers

It never ceases to amaze me that people find time to read. The demographics for TV viewing don't seem to leave more than a few minutes for anything else. And yet, bookstores are growing at the rate of ten percent a year. Book publishing flourishes. Public library circulation is booming, and bookstores in urban centers stay open until midnight. Unfortunately, this is not true in all countries. Not everywhere are people at liberty to read whatever they wish; many books are simply not available.

We are aware of trade deficits, but not as they apply to books. Our country exports far too few books to compete in "the war of ideas." The democratic process depends on the dissemination of ideas. In the plural, not just one point of view. The Soviet Union sows its message abroad through books far more intensively than we do. In 1984, the United States Information Agency exported only 600,000 books: less than five percent of the 12½ million distributed in 1955. In 1979, the Soviets produced 87 million books translated into other languages, most of them for export. A Library of Congress study stated the issues succinctly: "A book costs less, lasts longer, and penetrates more deeply than any other means of international communication of information and ideas. Books influence public opinion and even political doctrine." In the past twenty years, fifty USIA libraries in foreign countries have been closed. The pen is mightier than the sword. But the microphone is mightier than the pen, particularly when no printed word is available to be studied, analyzed, discussed, questioned, and quoted. Discussion, the axle grease of democracy, is much more effective when literary documentation can be used as a basis. Reading allows time for thinking. "It's time for the United States to enter the competition of ideas. If not, then little by little, mind by mind, other attitudes will prevail."

I cannot imagine life without books. I have had a long-standing love affair with the world between hard covers. Becoming eligible for my first library card is a most vivid childhood memory. Loving books starts early. Preschool. Prekindergarten. Prenatal? Some think it does; intense young mothers-to-be now read *Alice in Wonderland* to their gestating future bookworms.

Part of the charm and enduring quality of Lewis Carroll's *Adventures* are those improbable surprises. Not long ago, one more was added when the original wood engravings suddenly materialized. They were found in two metal boxes, one of them marked simply "Alice." It is hard to believe that they had been forgotten in the cool, dark vault of a London bank, and reemerged in perfect condition.

The wood blocks, made for Sir John Tenniel's illustrations, disappeared years ago. No one at the publisher's knew what had become of them. The author himself inquired by letter in 1867: "By the way, who has the wood blocks? I can hardly doubt that they're being carefully kept. But, considering the sum I had to pay for them, I shall be glad to be certain that they're safe from all possibility of damage." And so they were!

It was said of Charles Lutwidge Dodgson that "he was a great fusspot. He was always anxious about things and would have been reassured" to see how well the printing blocks were kept. For his sake, I'm glad he never knew no one knew where that was! British banks allow customers to bring in their own locked boxes, of all shapes and sizes. Before the twentieth century, there was no fee for storage. Perhaps that explains how two locked boxes, containing ninety-two carefully wrapped and individually tagged printing blocks, resurfaced in mint condition after more than a hundred years. After the excitement of finding the originals of the characters that populate the stories of Lewis Carroll, the precious blocks are again down—down in the vault.

Novels, mysteries, romances, children's books, biographies are but sidelines to the profusion of advice, information, analysis, and encouragement to be found in books. There is hardly a subject of concern that does not get rewritten and updated each year. How did the human race evolve socially, emotionally, physically, technically, financially before how-to books? I suspect they did it the way nature intended: by learning from each other. Instead, we read about "Marriage Management," "Homefront Budget Battle," "Role Reversal," "Real Estate, the Real Escape" and, of course, "Computer Competence." There probably was a book on child rearing before Dr. Spock. But I don't think my mother or grandmother had one. Instead, they had blank-paged diaries, with beautifully tooled leather bindings. In these, they kept their own counsel concerning marriage, accounts, and their children's progress: how they grew; what they ate; when they rolled over, sat up, had the measles, got the first tooth. They also recorded the astoundingly clever things tots did and said. Now, that makes good reading!

The Superintendent of the Chicago Public Schools, Ruth Love, predicts "if we could get parents to read to their preschool children, fifteen minutes a day, we could revolutionize the schools." Jim Trelease has gone one step further; he's written the ultimate how-to book on books, *The Read Aloud Handbook:* * a guide to awaken the child's desire to read and instill a love for literature. Along the way, we learn about a new problem, defined as *aliteracy.* It identifies that vast group of Americans who are literate but unmotivated to read. They can't be bothered. They have no reason to do it. Technological gadgetry informs them and entertains them. Many manage to earn a living without having to read. Over ninety-eight percent of households in this country have that marvel of modern life: a TV set.

Aliteracy has a serious side effect. Not reading means not thinking clearly. When the respect for language is lost, an inadequate working vocabulary makes it virtually impossible to formulate a point of view, much less defend it in dialogue. It impairs the ability to reason. Reading, like anything else, must be practiced, or the skill will diminish in time. We graduate three million youngsters from high schools every year, but many consider reading a nuisance. When the California Department of Education polled sixthgraders, seventy percent of them said they rarely read for pleasure. Not all the blame falls in any one place, school or home. Yet children who are read to early in life by responsive adults will be early readers. They will learn to love the printed word and continue to feel a need to read. Their counterparts will be anti-intellectuals. Are parents taking their children to the video cassette rental place for membership before they get them a library card?

Public libraries are less spiritual and awe-inspiring than they used to be; more businesslike, frenetic, and automated. The stacks of wooden card-catalogue drawers, with brass pulls that hook comfortably over the index finger, are becoming obsolete. Remember the hushed sound when they glide out, the confident click when you push them back? The smell of the wood, brass, and paper. The orderliness. The dog-eared index cards to research homework, science projects, book reports. Reference drawers now are antiques. Computerization is replacing them.

Historically, libraries were the locus of learning, the repository of knowledge, the meeting ground for intellectual exchange. Ephesus, that ancient Greek city (now part of Turkey), prided itself in its library. The treasures it contained were as precious as any in temples and palaces. Now, I hear the world has too many books. Apparently 800,000 books and 900,000 periodicals, as well as untold numbers of other important documents are published each year around the globe. Informational overload! One solution will be to pool resources and space in a national and international network. Yale University's library system contains close to 9 million books, as well as 2¼ million rare books. Although it adds only seven or eight percent of the world's new literature each year, that still comes to four or five million new books! Would microfilm be the answer? Well, first it's difficult to study that way. Second, the conversion costs about forty-five dollars per volume (added to the twenty dollars or more the book costs). As children, we learn that library means sharing books. Now, libraries must share. Librarian is no longer an ivory-tower profession. It's a job for technocrats.

Since I've been a member of the performing arts for eighty years, you might assume that I am delighted that people prefer to receive their entertainment and education by being spectators. But I am all too aware of the importance of reading, effortlessly. It may surprise you to learn that the United States is not at the top of the list of literate countries. On the contrary, we fall far below several other nations. I, like most of my contemporaries, was read to when I was very young—and even later on, when studying theatrical roles. My love for literature started then. And so it was for my own children. Some of my fondest memories of our family life are of the bedtime-story readings and the Sunday afternoon sharing of funny and fascinating articles from the paper. What will you buy for Christmas? Do the children on your list receive pen and pencil sets? Books? Stationery?

Dr. Seuss, through whose amusing children's literature so many have been stimulated, says "you really can't teach reading as a science. Love gets mixed into it." A story about a teddy bear makes a greater impact when the child hugs the stuffed toy, while the parent holds the child and the book. Is this only for toddlers? Not at all. It should never stop, not until the child reaches the point in intellectual development when the desire to read is strong enough to become a compulsion.

Maurice Sendak is one of the favorite writers of children's books. This author/artist has an approach to childhood very different from the ordinary. It is not based, as one might expect, on thorough research and extensive contact with children. On the contrary. A lonely childhood, his own, is the well from which springs his superstimulated imagination and his fantastic cast of characters, whose adventures he illustrates so charmingly.

He had an overprotective mother, who was so concerned about his health that she rarely let him play with other children—not even his own brother and sister. He observed life through the window of his room and gathered into his solitary existence the most outrageous characters, events, and happenings. A child's need to set forth into the unknown happens again and again in his stories. He knew what it was to be a virtual prisoner. Loneliness, fear, frustration, anger are played out in words and pictures. "From their earliest years, children live with disruptive emotions . . . they continuously cope with frustration as best they can. It is through fantasy that children achieve catharsis . . . the natural inclination of children is to be happy." Sendak's books are ideal because childhood reading is the basis for adult reading, and that *is* what shapes people.

The world is too much with today's children. Atoms explode in their living rooms and bodies ooze out their life on the rug in front of the TV. Along comes the "Mark Twain Controversy." According to a school administrator, *Huckleberry Finn* is a racist story!!—"a book about dishonesty, dumbness, and inhumanity." Columnist Russell Baker's opinion is that "this is the kind of risk you invite when you assign books of some subtlety to youngsters mentally unprepared to enjoy them." And, I might add, when you have literature taught by people who are unequipped to teach it. Baker says that much of what we consider classical literature is not to be read before we are thirty-five. I would be delighted if no one ever made another television miniseries based on classic literature. Most people have not touched these books since some eager teacher spoiled it all for them. Turn off the TV tonight and read Dickens, or Twain, or Shakespeare. You may realize, with astonishment, that you have really never read them before.

Bookstores, record shops, and teachers have a new competitive arena in which to grapple for the American mind: talking books. It is the hot topic at booksellers' conventions. Hundreds of taped books are already available. This is fast food—for the mind. Pop a literary version of a TV dinner into a cassette player and, instead of spending a week with Mark Twain or a few evenings with Dr. Zhivago, we are treated to literature and classics in flash-frozen condensation. In two hours, Wendy Hiller gives you *Jane Eyre,* or Derek Jacobi reads *1984.* Amazing as it may seem, such high-talent presentations of fine writings cost less than ten dollars, abridged of course. Full-length versions can run twenty hours or more, and cost around seventy-five dollars. Hurrying to your library may be a waste of time; most cassettes are out on loan.

Jonathan Kozol, author of *Illiterate America,* † is not at all happy with the idea of children listening, with headsets, to highly abridged versions of our literary heritage. Novelist John Hersey says "Condensation leaves me very much aghast. The minute you start subtracting, bias sets in." The columnist George F. Will has no objection to full-length book cassettes. He said he "jogged all the way through World War II with Winston Churchill's six-volume history." Mr. Kozol worries that "tapes are one more disincentive to literacy." Listening is toil-free—no effort, no time to stop and think, to reread. What about sweet, soothing solitude and the "silence that surrounds reading?" Are we a society where no one wants to hear the sound of his own thoughts? Wired heads are listening everywhere. I have yet to see one laugh, grin, or cry.

* *Read Aloud Handbook,* Jim Trelease, Penguin Books, New York, 1985
† *Illiterate America,* Jonathan Kozol, Anchor Press, Doubleday & Company, Inc., Garden City, New York, 1985

Behave Yourself

When I was first practicing my social skills in New York, at the age of twenty or so, I felt I needed something to give me a sense and a look of importance, worldliness, sophistication, culture. I went to the library and chose a book on Japanese prints, of all things! I waded through that book to familiarize myself with tongue-twisting names and art forms; I memorized them all and became really quite glib on the subject. But I never got a chance to demonstrate my depth of knowledge. The minute I started to expound my Far Eastern cultural wisdom to table partners, a glaze would come over their eyes and I learned quickly to drop the subject.

What's wrong with most casual conversations is that we try so hard not to be casual. We feel obliged to come up with something to make us sound interesting, feel special. The unusual weather. An illness or demise. Pains, aches. Landlord. Government. Name the thorn of your choice. Could we learn to live more completely if we concentrated on the ordinary instead of the extraordinary? In an essay on the subject, Cynthia Ozick quotes Henry James: "We are all under sentence of death . . . we have an interval, and then our place knows us no more . . . our only chance lies in expanding that interval, in getting as many pulsations as possible into the given time." Does that mean we should cram our lives full of extraordinary experiences? Ozick doesn't think so. What really matters to her "is first noticing, and then sanctifying the Ordinary." But, most of us curse the repetitiveness of daily life, don't we?

To be "observant": the word has religious overtones. And so it should. Observant, in the physical sense of gathering in everything our five senses can absorb, is more directly a celebration of life than taking notice of remarkable events. Seeing the most fanciful floral arrangement of exotic blossoms can never compete with watching a crocus push up through the snow. An artist brings to creativity a synthesis of the common, the mundane—sifted through a special talent for distillation. We feel sanctimonious looking at or listening to this creation, but go away with a sense of frustration. We don't really get it! It seems simplistic or convoluted with complications. It's not our view of the world. And what is our view?

If we persist in glorifying only the outstanding, noticing only the extraordinarily beautiful or ugly, we're neither really living nor truly observant, in both senses of the word. "The ordinary," says Cynthia Ozick, "is the divine."

Much of what we must do routinely, or want to do, loses its appeal. Only the unusual is exciting, only what's different is amusing. Only newness is stimulating. One can achieve that by simply scrambling one's timetable. If you never go for a walk at six in the morning, you won't see the Canadian geese fly in formation. You won't know that fog smells clean. You can't fantasize about the milk wagon of long ago. If you never turn on the radio in the middle of the night, you never find out what the swing shift listens to, what is broadcast for the lost and the lonely. If you never eat breakfast in a truck stop, you'll never hear other opinions. If you never sit on a bench in the park at dusk, you can't learn about the light painters see or the sounds poets hear.

A change in routine heightens awareness. Don't call Aunt

Sophie this week. Call Uncle Morris, who'd love to hear from you. You sit in the same chair, to read the same publications. Read in the library—a volume or magazine you've never heard of. Take your lunch break near a school yard; the music of play will overwhelm you with nostalgia. Does your social life center around Saturday night? Make it Sunday brunch; people look different in the sunlight. Do you take your vacation in the summer, at the beach? Switch to snow-covered mountains at a lodge with a wood-burning fireplace. If your holiday table has been graced by the same set of relatives forever, call them and say "not this year," and then go visit a friend whose invitation you turned down for years. You see the world in a new light when you get up at a different hour.

Why do we all spend so much time and emotion on uncontrollable events and unalterable facts? Catch snatches of conversation—in a restaurant, elevator, at a party—and most likely, the gist of the grousing is about things beyond changing. I wish I could wear that style, but I'm too short-waisted. Isn't it hot . . . cold . . . windy . . . dreary . . . You name it, everyone is against the weather. According to a professor of clinical psychiatry, "our thoughts, not external events, create unhappiness. Negative thoughts distort the actual situation so that even relatively minor disappointments can trigger a disproportionately black mood."* It isn't necessary to cultivate a Pollyanna attitude, which would not allow us to acknowledge disappointments, normal anger or grief, anxiety and guilt. All of these emotional reactions to life's imperfections are perfectly normal—but within reason! If we let them dominate, we are doomed to a life of negatives.

Dr. David Burns teaches "cognitive" thinking. With that, his patients are able to combat negative feelings and can alter self-defeating behavior and thought processes. We ourselves are responsible for how we feel about the things that happen to us. In a way, it's true that "what we don't know won't hurt us." This may be simplistic, but just imagine you didn't know your boss had reviewed your performance record last week (and you made out okay). Had you been aware of this, your mental acrobatics would have twisted you into a pretzel for days.

We depress ourselves by self-deprecation. Much of the disapproval we think is directed against us is, in fact, self-inflicted. It's possible to develop better control over our moods with more understanding, logic, and insight. No one can alter the inevitable—nor the past. But, we can change how we feel about ourselves. And we can do it *today*.

* "You Can Change The Way You Feel," by Dr. David Burns, *Ladies' Home Journal,* June 1982

Time Frames

What would you call the most significant day in your life? If you're letting a memory album of brief images float by to find the answer, you are looking in the wrong direction. The most important day in your life is today. Second in line is (you've got the idea), tomorrow. If today is inconsequential, you are cheating yourself. It is not any one thing or event that gives this day special status. It's your day. You do it. Winning the lottery would do it for you? Well, it is a harmless game, except to those who believe in it and get hooked. Not you, eh? I went for an early morning walk once and found a ten-dollar bill on the grass, drenched with dew. Now, wasn't that a surprise, an omen almost. This is going to be a good day! What do you suppose I did the next few mornings, as I went for my ritual brisk walk? Looked to see if there was another greenback, growing unnoticed. I admit it, I was hooked.

What is wrong with state lotteries and the hype they engender are the astronomical sums people hope to win. Millions of dollars. That is not a prize. It is more like taking on the job of Atlas. Winning a few hundred or thousand dollars, that would be amusing. It cannot change your life or become an unfamiliar burden. Just enough to give yourself a nice treat and rekindle the belief in your luck. That belief is much more valuable than all the promises of a million-dollar windfall. We are a people whose democratic ideals assure us that everyone can be upwardly mobile—if we work for it.

One can trace the development of how we live by choosing just one word on which to build a portrait. "Attached," for example. How wonderful it was to move from tenements to a semiattached (two- or four-family) dwelling! Later, the family (whose grandfather still tells of the detached privy), advances to a private home with the added luxury of an attached garage. They have arrived, in suburbia. The aim today is to create as many additional attachments to that estatelet as the law will allow. Walls and roofs are pushed up and out in a frenzy of acquisitions and mergers. Eventually, the move is back to a semiattached two- or three-story dwelling, called a townhouse—out of town. The talk about grown children quite recently still was of grudgingly approved attachments and hopes for brilliant marriages.

Now, parental party patter is a torrent of college and career accomplishments that make mothers and fathers sparkle in reflected glory. Their personal attachments are glossed over. The older generation may have gotten used to the loosely woven fidelity of their children, but they still lack an adequate vocabulary to make it fit their own (official) mores. Son- or daughter-in-love defines the status of the current connection.

Globe-Trotting

"Tell me about your vacation." Now, there's a request most of us hesitate to formulate. Folks just love telling all kinds of boring details and will rarely tell you the negatives. Sitting on a dune, staring at the ocean. Lying in a deck chair, reading a trashy novel. Eating too much. Meeting no one interesting. Fishing, but what for? Well, it's better than working. Except for people who spend their vacations in places chosen by Earthwatch: they have a job to do. Earthwatch, of Belmont, Massachusetts, matches scientific research with volunteers who want to help. For charges ranging from $450 to $2,500 plus transportation costs, this nonprofit organization sends volunteers on two weeks of scientific research. The cost to the amateur science buff is tax deductible. Volunteers provide manpower for time-consuming, tedious work, which usually requires no special skills and yet is invaluable to scientists.

"When I'm on vacation, I want to be doing something as different as I can from my everyday life. Earthwatch is about as far away from that as you can get," said a retired banker. She has been rescuing the eggs of giant turtles when they waddle ashore in the dead of night. Sometimes the exhausted turtle deposits a hundred eggs the size of billiard balls. But if they're too close to the ocean, the tide will smash them. Earthwatch volunteers are trained to move the eggs, monitor their hatching with a stethoscope, protect them from predators—including man—and measure and tag the mother. (The father never comes ashore.) Earthwatchers come from all walks of life with a special love for our planet—the less touristy side of it.

Sailors and actors learn to live out of trunks; it eliminates all options. Packing for a trip is no one's favorite pastime. I have known people who hire someone to do it for them. That way, at least they can't blame themselves for mistakes in judgment. Traveling easy begins with a talent for selectiveness. Don't look in your closet to find out what you want to take. You will take too much if you tempt yourself that way. Instead, make a list of the days you will be away and the special events. Then fill in the clothes you need for the first two days. Look down the list to see when you can wear each item a second and third time. You get the idea? Don't digress when you start to pack; don't include all kinds of alternatives and "what ifs." Remember the last time! You carried the luggage yourself most of the time. You used only half of what you hauled around. You don't need more than you can move easily on a luggage tote. Forget elegance while in transit. Only the infrequent traveler still tries to look like a page from a magazine. The experienced are prepared for long waits, long corridors, long nights.

Before I became an experienced traveler (when I was still quite young, wasn't well known yet, and had not ever been on television), I went to Philadelphia one day. A taxi took me to Pennsylvania Station and when I got there, I found I had forgotten my purse at home. I didn't have a cent and no time to go back. I exploded to the driver, "I can't pay you. I haven't got any money. I can't even get on the train." Unbelievable as it may be, he gave me money for my ticket to Philadelphia. He had no idea who I was; he just was a good man, a caring, generous soul.

To the details that go into preparing for travel, one must

now add a trip to the library or other location where a photocopy machine is available. It is wise to Xerox all travel papers and documents and the contents of one's wallet. Pickpockets are proliferating like guppies in a pond. Travelers come home with stories that used to make amusing films, but are now everyday, everywhere, everyone's tale of woe. The rules of the road don't apply only to the Casbah. No. The Place Vendôme in Paris. The circular roadway around Rome's Colosseum. London's Piccadilly Circus. New York's Greenwich Village. Gangs of gypsy children in rags, elegantly dressed con artists, pickpockets with class or with bedbugs—the traveler is their easy prey while occupied with picture-taking, pointing, staring, shopping, or climbing over language barriers. Once our attention is diverted from purse or wallet, camera or luggage, someone else is latching on.

Don't leave home without copies of valuable documents, credit cards, identification, and passport. Purse snatchers will most likely throw all of it in the trash can. It is currency and traveler's checks they need. You, on the other hand, will be desperate without the rest of it. First step: Don't bring with you what you don't need—Social Security card, irreplaceable photos. (Probably two-thirds of what is in your wallet.) Leave your tickets and most of your cash in the hotel safe. Photocopies of stolen originals will save monumental hassles at police stations, airline desks, and consulates. Settle on one credit card, and keep it separate from cash and traveler's checks. It may surprise you to hear that carrying a shoulder bag slung across the chest is deemed dangerous by Paris police; they have seen folks dragged by thieves on motor scooters. If you feel yourself pushed in a crowd, you may be in a squeeze play between a pickpocket and an assistant. Grab for your wallet and make a ruckus if necessary. Chances are they will drop the loot, rather than risk a confrontation.

If you have never gone through the unpleasantness of a lost piece of luggage, you are either a stay-at-home or carry all your possessions on your back. It is inevitable that one

day, the airline of your choice will transport you to your
intended destination and your personal belongings else-
where. To be parted from your baggage raises a particular
outrage because one gives so much thought and time to
putting into that valise only what one absolutely needs and
wants. But did you really put enough thought into packing?
Where did you put your jewelry? Good grief, it's in that
grip! Maybe a thief spied it, clearly outlined as the suitcase
underwent its requisite X-ray scanning. So, now it's gone.

That is how I learned to travel with imitation baubles. I
was going out to Los Angeles for a personal appearance. I
took my good pearls and some other valuable pieces, to
make a splash with the movie people. Of course, theirs were
far more spectacular than mine could ever hope to be. My
treasures were minuscule in comparison. The one piece of
luggage that went astray contained all of it. Twenty-four
hours of sheer hell waiting for word from that airline! I got
it back, but the fright left a lasting impression, making a
confirmed costume jewelry devotee of me. I carry comfortable imitations.

If you're traveling to the tropics from your native, snow-
bound region, expect to spend the first day in winter wool-
lies if your carry-on bag did not contain shirt, shorts, and
sandals. To stack the odds in your favor in the game of lost
and found, clearly identify bags and parcels with secure,
indelible tags. A thoughtful friend supplies me with brightly
colored wool tassels, which make it easier for foreign por-
ters to help locate my belongings. By the way, theft is rare;
criminals don't like to do laundry, I guess. If you own baggage that could snap open or break, you are "packing up
your troubles in an old kit bag" and will have very little to
smile about.

Airlines reimburse you up to $750 for each piece of lost
luggage on a domestic flight. If your luggage and content
exceed that limit, you'd be wise to have receipts (and photographs) of valuable items, so that you could make a claim
against your homeowner's insurance. You also can buy "ex-
cess-valuation" insurance from the airline. If you don't want

to spend the first few hours after arrival racking your memory to list what was lost, perhaps you should have prepared an inventory of contents. But that's looking at the bleak side, isn't it?

Lost luggage is an inevitability. I have lost mine in every capital of the world except Peking—because I haven't been there, yet. Once, when I landed in Paris my luggage went on to London. It was late at night when I checked into my favorite hotel, The Lancaster. Dear Mr. Wolf, the proprietor, greeted me in the lobby. My face was a picture of fury and despair. He asked what was wrong. When I told him he snapped his fingers and gave an order in unintelligibly rapid French. When I got to my room, there on the bed were his pajamas. The trouble was, I'm five feet tall and he is six-something. I trailed those pants legs behind me like a Kabuki dancer.

Who would plunk down several thousand dollars for something they have never seen? Travelers. All one gets to see in advance of taking a tour are tempting brochures filled with hyperbole and irresistible color photos. Rooms and cabins always look to be the size of the Hall of Mirrors at Versailles. Buffet splendor appears to stretch fifty feet. All servants smile, their hands folded *behind* their backs. Thus, travelers are lured into unknown, prepaid, nonrefundable packaged pleasure. Venturing out into the world *should* be full of surprises. The right kind of surprises. Not the unexpected, all too frequent horrors: inadequate accommodations, far below what was promised; additional expenses not anticipated; scheduling that is too rushed or not well programmed. One must know what questions to ask. "All-inclusive" price. Is that for land arrangements only? "Air fare included." Does that mean from *your* city, or is there an add-on fare? Service charges, taxes, exit fees, weekend surcharges, high-season supplements. Ask about possible costs "over and beyond." Solo travelers sometimes must pay a supplement if they wish to room alone. Be sure you realize which sites listed are to be actually visited, and which are merely stopovers or driven through. The questions go on and on. There is no such thing as a silly question! It just requires a little homework. *At home*, before you go!

Here is a multiple choice question. Vacation is

    a) restful solitude
    b) novelty and excitement
    c) sights and culture
    d) sports and exertion

If there are two of you, the correct answers would probably be a, b, c, and d. And therein lies a bit of a problem. Whether you are married, with decades of travel experience, or traveling with a friend, proceed cautiously! This is particularly true if you are planning to go someplace you have never been or taking a new tack, such as a shipboard vacation. Two people, no matter how well they know each other, have very different needs, tolerances, and habits. When togetherness is a twenty-four-hour, seven-day, or twenty-one-day affair and lacking some, if not all, the comforts of home, problems can arise. Food habits are disrupted; sleep cycles are disturbed; weather influences each one differently.

When traveling with someone, take large doses of patience and tolerance with your morning coffee. If she wants to shop, don't go along if you hate it. Go to a ball game when you don't want to see another ruin. If African art isn't your thing, meet later for lunch. If one wants night life and the other is knocked out by nine, take an afternoon nap— but go at least once. Work out the finances in advance. Married or companions, with other friends or on an organized tour, money matters should not become an issue. Don't argue about tips and prices. Travel with people whose budgets are more or less equal. Sharing a room or a cabin with a stranger is very difficult; unless you are the soul of patience, I advise against it. Try to keep a lighthearted attitude. It's a bad time to discuss long-standing, deep-seated problems. You left home to have a good time. To have a good time, leave home out of it.

Anxious Move

There was a time in my life when I decided that my house, Pretty Penny, was more of a burden than a pleasure. So I sold it. I thought I was taking a very mature attitude about the whole matter of uprooting and replanting myself. But it just so happened that the buyer caught the same case of cold feet as I did at the very same moment and we managed to cancel out each other's giant steps.

There are so many people whose homes have taken on the appearance of a huge dollar sign. They read the real-estate pages looking for the current market value in their area and realize that their original $20,000 to $30,000 investment could easily net them four times that much. What would that buy them now? Not a palace, to be sure. Perhaps a one-room condo and cold storage for a lot of warm memories.

Curbside and cocktail conversations among longtime neighbors seem to concentrate heavily on who got what for his house and how their young marrieds can't find even a so-called "starter house" for under eighty. You notice no one bothers to clarify "eighty" by adding "thousand dollars." What I found out when I made that almost irrevocable step of selling Pretty Penny is that a house is not a financial investment. It is part of you. Your fingerprints are on the garden soil. Your life is painted on the walls. Every step you have ever taken is etched on those floors. The dreams you dreamed are just outside the windows. The tears you shed are still on the glass. Does one hear voices there? Of course, and be glad of it. Can you sometimes not go into a room because memories will overwhelm you? Yes, but better than none at all. Those unused dishes remind us of parties we no longer give, and the dining room is too big now. But the house is just the right size to hold the past. And that's how I like it.

Moving is not always done by choice. Relocation is an American tradition. Corporate executives go through it periodically. Our ancestors escaped the fatherland to come here; young people just try to find a way to leave mother. When moving was easier and cheaper, a lot of folks annually picked up stakes (for some reason, on the fifteenth of October) to find a new apartment. They considered this drastic step easier than having the painters come to redecorate the old one. Another incentive was the "concession" landlords used to give—a rent-free month or two. Can you imagine!

Moving is unavoidable at certain times in our lives. We go away to school. We marry. We get a promotion. We double in number. We need less space again. We are alone once more. We can no longer stay alone. Each time, it is traumatic. We feel a loss when we must leave old friends, familiar neighborhoods, storekeepers; but we are not always aware of these emotions until after we have moved, settled in, unpacked, rearranged, and gotten past that very busy time. It is then that anxiety sets in; we must recognize it and make ourselves even busier to overcome it. To avoid the shock of relocating, understand beforehand that you will need time to readjust. Learn as much as possible about the new location to mitigate the left-out, lost, and unfamiliar feelings.

Company of One

We all have things in common when it comes to feeling lonely and forlorn. We do not know how to talk about it. We are usually a little ashamed, even angry. Somehow, we get the notion that we are not supposed to feel lonely, that it is our own fault. We experience a sense of guilt.

Feeling uncomfortably alone or deserted has little to do with age, family, or social position. You can be married, have loving children, a close circle of friends, and still there are days when an unexplained, unreasonable sense of abandonment overtakes you. To whom can we talk about it? If you speak to your mate, you give the impression of dissatisfaction and petulance. If you mention it to your children, you appear to be demanding and possessive. If you admit it to your friends, you make them feel inadequate and uncaring. Should you speak of it at all? Yes, but it is not easy.

Consolation will seem to be inappropriate, advice patronizing. It does not help to be told "everyone feels that way sometimes." There is little comfort in well-intentioned advice to "keep yourself busier," "join a club," "take a course," "get a job," "make new friends." Coming home to an empty house is unbearable to most people. It *is* a condition of life—for the school child, the divorced, the widowed.

Loneliness can become an illness if dwelled on unnaturally or compensated for with liquor or drugs or overeating. It is easier to cope with if recognized as a normal, common occurrence, which is usually temporary. Therapy can help if the feeling of despair is chronic and self-criticism is added to hopelessness. Being alone is not to be equated with loneliness. Nor is being with people a guarantee against it; quite the contrary, especially at large gatherings. Recognize it for what it is—inevitable! Do not let it get the better of you. Nothing is forever—not marriage, not family, not friends. New companionship is more readily attainable if we don't try to think of it in terms of a lifetime.

We grow up the day we are allowed to go somewhere alone and don't have to call home to say we arrived. It may seem we wish to teach children independence, but in fact we train them not to be alone. From the very beginning, the child alone in his sandbox either has a playmate planted next to him or is yanked out and sent off to nursery school. There he is taught group interaction! We are not given sufficient opportunities, nor do we make an effort to enjoy our own companionship. And then one day, it is too late to learn. It is a good idea to start early to practice aloneness and learn to become comfortable with singleness in this paired-off world. It is not always economics but psychology that leads the single person to eat in a diner or pizza parlor, even if a French restaurant would be preferable. "A table for one, please" is difficult to say.

Researchers are documenting that loneliness might hasten our demise. They are not sure why it affects mortality. But perhaps like other thought processes that are linked to our physiological well-being, loneliness is a state of mind. Although friendship definitely has a beneficial effect on health, we should become acquainted with solitude as a challenge. Yes, you *can* buy a new winter coat without your friend. It is marvelous to spend an afternoon alone on the beach. I assure you no one stares if you go to the movies by yourself. Are you willing to admit you have never taken a trip by air alone? Most men feel anxious in an empty house, and women get the jitters in a hotel lobby. But, if you listen carefully, you really are never alone; there is a continuous conversation going on inside your head. You can control this chatter by switching to a positive channel: tune out gloom and doom, which somehow got programmed into us.

A Stop Along the Way

Health care is news, partly because of costs and partly because of length of life, both of which exceed expectation. Death is not much talked about, though all of us think about it. Dying used to take place at home, in your bed, among your relatives (unless a sudden calamity struck when one was away). Drawn curtains and subdued household sounds, involvement by the whole family. Children learned early what needed to be accepted as natural. The family who was about to suffer a loss was actively involved in the rite of passage; dying was made as bearable a release as possible. At about the same time that births were made safer in the sterile environment of hospitals, death, too, was relegated to the mechanical atmosphere of medical facilities. But hospitals are not necessarily the only or best place to care for the terminally ill or aged.

Death, as much a part of the human experience as birth, is treated by the medical profession as though it were an embarrassment, a sign of failure. Francis Bacon wrote "death is a friend of ours; and he who is not ready to entertain him is not at home." Of course, he meant that metaphysically. Yet it does point to the idea that we must, once again, learn to

understand that the end of life should be considered a part
of living, not to be shunted to the last room of the corridor
in the acute-care medical unit of an artificial environment.
In the last stages of a final illness, we need only the absence
of pain and the presence of family. Qualified hospices are
the practical, humane alternative to institutional care. Since
1979, when just ten such programs existed, hospice care has
expanded to more than 1,500 hospices in this country.
Modern pain therapy makes it easier to alleviate suffering,
which usually is felt less acutely in a more supportive setting. Fear and apprehension, rejection and alienation, mis-
information and emotional neglect are the terrors that be-
set institutionalized patients.

We are relearning that living and dying are not only in-
separable, but normal. In the motion picture *Terms of En-
dearment*, there is a tearful scene when the young mother,
dying of cancer in a hospital bed, makes her brave last
farewells. Her two little boys can barely speak to her: The
ten-year-old is tight-lipped and angry. The six-year-old
fights his tears, speechlessly. She dies in silence, in dehu-
manized surroundings. In contrast, I know of one elderly
woman who died at home, in the care and company of her
family. Her adult daughters took turns lying in her bed,
close to the mother they loved. It took three years for Medicare to see the wisdom of incorporating hospice organizations into the system. Now we may see some funds flowing
into it through government channels, but we must guard
against bureaucratic requirements and regulations that may
serve to undermine the concept. Hospice care is extremely
cost-efficient, with savings of as much as forty percent over
institutionalization. In spite of this, the new Medicare pay-
ment rate for routine home care has been cut. Is there a
confusion somewhere about disposable dollars and disposable people?

A hospice is sometimes just a room or a wing, occasionally a building; but usually it is home care. The specially
trained staff considers the family of the patient as important
as IVs or opiates. Hospitals are not geared to the dying. The

officious attitude of some hospital personnel has its counterparts in the feelings of denial of the dying patient and the
false hopes and brave front put up by the family. Once it
becomes evident that a patient cannot recover, the routin-
ized hospital setting, and its resulting cold treatment,
should be abandoned whenever possible. Hospice personnel direct their efforts not to curing, but to caring. The
family needs help; the patient needs love. Fear, pain, loss,
anxiety, anger, frustration, time, and money are factors
both the dying and the living must cope with and learn to
understand. Time spent together, in honest openness,
makes it all so much easier to accept.

Putting Death on Hold

In his ninth novel, *The Dean's December,* Nobelist Saul Bellow addresses himself to, among other things, death and dying. He suggests that really every other day is a day of dying, if we could only see it. And if we, as a society, could learn to accept this, we might agree with Stewart Alsop, who said shortly before his own death, "A dying man needs to die, as a sleeping man needs to sleep, and there comes a time when it is wrong, as well as useless, to resist."

Health care today has taken on more than it can handle— the extension of life beyond all reason. Unfortunately, somewhere along the line it always seems to come down to money. One percent of the gross national product is spent on the dying in the last few weeks of life. If, instead of useless heroic efforts, this meant that they were made as comfortable and free of pain as possible, there would be no question that that is right and no expense should be spared. To the astronomical amounts spent to keep people from their heaven add the ever-increasing premiums doctors and hospitals pay to protect themselves. The specter of mal- practice suits hangs over them for every measure they take —or choose not to take. Fees are accordingly increased,

raising the bill, which in most cases is not paid by citizens—
well not directly, anyway. We are caught in a spiral. "If we
are to do anything about this problem, we must educate the
public on the limits of medicine. Physicians, disciplined by
the threat of malpractice and an honorable code of ethics,
usually do too much. Most important, we must understand
that we are on this earth for a limited time."*

Isn't it strange that even the oldest among us avoid the
subject. We don't talk about it to our families, but we
should. More emphatically, we must! How will they know
what to do if we have never expressed our personal "end
game" philosophy? Or is it that we never formulate it?

As for myself, I am quite at peace about the whole thing.
At times I look forward to death, not morbidly or despon-
dently; on the contrary, I love life. At other times I say to
myself: now this has gone on long enough. It's time for a
change. A change is what I do really believe it to be. It is not
possible for me to think that God, or nature, could create
great minds and spirits that have inhabited this earth and
then would snuff them out. Long ago, in my formative
years, a line from J. M. Barrie's *Peter Pan* took hold in my
head: "To die will be an awfully big adventure." I love to
travel, and that will be just one more trip—the most memorable one, no doubt.

I don't know when terror of death came upon us. It was
not there in the Middle Ages. For centuries, the end of life
was considered an elaborate, formal, beautiful occasion.
Now it is full of anguish and unnatural extension. Science
blurs the distinction between mortality and immortality.

The subject of dying is frequently in the news—how elderly, devoted couples end their lives together, and where
the road takes the neglected, ill, poor, and alone. It is not
uncommon for ill people to hoard medicine. They fill their
prescriptions but prefer to suffer rather than to take them,
so that when the time comes when they are deemed "terminal," they have the means to end their lives.

The Association for the Right to Die with Dignity held an
international conference in France to consider new points

of view in the face of medical advances. "For too long, people have been unwilling to talk about death, so that hidden fears add immensely to physical suffering." What is against the laws of nature—inserting tubes into every passage of a dying human body or withdrawing and withholding such extraordinary means? We cannot continue to adhere to the old convictions that a physician's duty is to preserve life at all cost. We must allow ourselves to recognize the new circumstances, that medical knowledge provides the possibility of virtually simulating life where, in reality, it exists no longer.

Euthanasia remains illegal. The columnist Flora Lewis writes: "Judges are scarcely better equipped than others to rule on the consequences of progress in medicine that has vastly increased life expectancy and heightened the ordeal of death in many cases." It is inhumane to prolong dying under the guise of maintaining life. The right to a good death is inalienable. A "living will," documenting your wishes on the use of "extraordinary measures" to sustain your life, is still not recognized as a legal document in every state.

Longevity is a miracle of modern medicine. Antibiotics have turned away the "old man's friend," pneumonia; pacemakers keep hearts tuned. We keep the frail elderly in medical institutions to their dying day, instead of among their relatives. Do you agree that few of us see death before we are fully grown—and many of us not even then? We treat the inevitable as though we could avoid it by looking away. (Most of us never see a birth, either; not even that of our own children.) "She's in a family way" is how we once described the beginning of a new life. The Germans say "she's in other circumstances." Leaving this world is couched in even more circumspect phrasing to avoid calling it by its real name.

Katharine Hepburn made a dark comedy motion picture about dying, *Grace Quigley*. It took her eleven years to find acceptance for the script written by Martin Zweiback. She was determined to help change attitudes about aging and death: "Have you been inside any of those places where they put old people? Well I have and that's why I wanted to make this movie. I think it's terribly important. I think when the body goes, or the mind goes, and it's time to say good-bye, why shouldn't you?" Miss Quigley, tired and old, hires a hit man to end her life and, in the process, finds a whole community of senior citizens who think as she does. Katharine says being occupied with love and work is what keeps you going, and she points to the importance of developing and retaining a sense of humor—even about death. She thinks "we're finally at that point." Not yet, Kate. But perhaps your film will help.

Not enough attention is paid to the rising statistic of suicides by elderly Americans, a rate that is more than fifty percent above that of the general population. One need not look beyond the front page of the morning paper to become aware of some of the underlying reasons. Federal cuts in Medicare, Medicaid, and food stamps. Fear of the future based on technology and on chemical and atomic devastation. Forced retirement sometimes due to corporate mergers, other times "encouraged" for the economic benefit of employers. Cutbacks in pensions and benefits. Downtrends in the financial market and the economy. "White men, especially if they are widowed or divorced, have the highest suicide rate of all. They are ten times as likely to commit suicide as women. The reason: When they retire, they have the farthest to fall and the experience is often devastating."†

Other reasons are aloneness or terminal illness. But depression may be the most severe affliction that tempts elderly people to look for a way out. Depression is a treatable condition, but it is too often not properly diagnosed. Doctors and health workers don't realize what it may mean to a man whose eyesight is failing when he is the only one to care for his disabled wife, or that the rising cost of medicine and insurance rates can be "the last straw." For those who moved to the Sunbelt, feeling cut off from family and friends can make life "not worth living." Are there answers?

Not unless *everyone* cares. The old social system is not applicable when life extends beyond one's financial means and can be extended beyond comfort, beyond endurance. Everyone should have a right to choose when, where, and how to die with dignity.

* Professor Fred McKinney, Brandeis University
† *The Wall Street Journal*, July 30, 1986

Widow Woman, Widow Man

"If there's anything I can do, let me know." I can think of no more well-meaning, heartfelt gesture; but it rarely receives the right response. We all have some difficulties expressing our feelings at a time of loss or tragedy in the life of others. So, we make what seems to be a really useful offer: "Call on me." "I want to be of help any way I can." But at a time of crisis and bereavement, few can think clearly enough to say what it is they need.

One way to make ourselves available and helpful is simply to be there. You will see for yourself where help can be offered, what needs to be done, and recognize opportunities to serve as a friend. Help with arrangements. Care for the children or the elderly. Board the dog. Clear up the kitchen. Handle the phone calls. There is nothing more important in this life than one human being reaching out to another. Sometimes, nothing more need be done than to brush a cheek thoughtfully with your fingertips. Deeds are so much easier than words.

We sometimes think it might be best not to mention the loss, hoping it will help the grieving forget. Actually, it is almost always better to do just the opposite. People want to know that this ended life has not been blotted out. They love to hear anecdotes and recalled conversations. It reassures them that they do not mourn alone, that their loved one is remembered by others, too. To accept what is irreversible is difficult, especially for the very young. Silence is not the way to go about it. To know someone has a place in the memory of others is important and comforting. Sending printed cards are, what I would call, obligatory offerings. Don't waste your time choosing an appropriately sentimental message. It takes much less time to write your thoughts, which surely will be more personal and appreciated. If you cannot think of a thing to write or say, choose a book as a token of your involvement. There are some for widows; others about loss and grief. Above all, continue to include your friend in your plans and social life, as you did before.

Widowers are an especially vulnerable group. Men do not expect to outlive their wives. A study conducted by the researchers at Johns Hopkins University found that a husband's death had almost no effect on the mortality rate of women, whereas older men are more likely to die within several years after their wives' deaths (in far greater numbers than married men of the same age). Bereaved women are expected to express their anguish and are allowed to conceal—no, draw attention to—it with inscrutable veils. Men must stand unprotected, stoic examples to their sons. Most men never contemplate living alone. Traditionally, women do. They have dozens of role models among their acquaintances in later life and among their relatives in early childhood. Their province is the home; it does not frighten them to be managing it on their own. Men are quite unprepared to find themselves alone; statistics, they thought, had been stacked against this possibility.

Women know how to cry. Men internalize their grief, which makes them much more susceptible to heart disease and ill health as a result of their bereavement. In good marriages, the man often relies entirely on his life's companion for emotional support, as a sounding board, and as recipient of his private thoughts and confidences. Most women have at least one other person with whom they share such a relationship.

One of the great revelations for an older man who suddenly finds himself widowed is the concept of dependency. Here he has gone through life, imagining that his wife was totally dependent on him; suddenly he realizes that he was equally dependent on her in all those everyday matters that he now finds so overwhelming. So, men remarry. And that is as it should be. It is easier for them because there are so many unmarried women. I just wish they would choose among their age group and leave the young things to their peers.

Who would have thought, a hundred years ago, that you could benefit from reading a book called *In Defense of Marriage*, or *Caring for Your Aging Parents*, or *Survival Handbook for Widows?* These subjects now must be learned from books. Previously, they were *experienced* in the home. When people lived and died in their home town, neighborhood, or farm, facts of life were *lived.* Understanding came from examples. "Coping," as it's called today, was learned from "role models," another one of those current terms—one that substitutes for mother, father, grandparent, aunt, cousin, teacher, preacher, and so forth. "Women outlive men by an average of sixteen years; three out of four married women can realistically expect to be widows, at least once."* Widowhood is one of those supreme shocks for which we are never prepared. "But too many women today lack the experience of having had others from whom to learn how to come to grips with grief. Picking up the pieces and planning a fulfilling new life should not be considered the rare exception."

I'm a bit self-conscious in talking about widowhood from my vantage point. I never seemed to need the usual kind of assistance and support. I had an ongoing, successful career. There was no real interruption in the natural flow of my life. This may hold true for today's career woman, too. But I see my contemporaries in a crisis state of disbelief when they find themselves bereft of the one person on whom they focused their lives. Not only were they devoted wives and housekeepers exclusively, they centered their pride on the male. He was the framework. They managed to go through life without ever seeing themselves as individuals, as complete human beings. And yet, in spite of my independence, my career, and even a second movie career, I felt diminished by half when Charlie died. I needed his advice, the security of talking with him, hearing him say perhaps what I thought but needed confirmed. I needed validation. It is a very wise thing for a woman to keep a high regard for her husband's intelligence and competence, even when she realizes, as we all do, that he is not quite the hero she thought he was.

If you stare at the word "alone," you can see "all one" in it. There *is* life after divorce or widowhood, even late in life. "What you take out of a divorce or a death is your *self*." A sermon in a single sentence. "In time, you'll redefine yourself."† There is nothing we can do about the blows fate deals us or our age at the time they strike. What we can do is acknowledge the need for self-preservation, the possibility that in this new phase, which is thrust upon us, we can develop into someone we never were before.

Face the probability of life's shocking events. This is not fiction. This is the future. Statistics point the way. The number of people over sixty-five will double by the year 2020; there will be 51 million. Fifteen million of them *now* are women; more than half are widows. The average age of widowhood is fifty-six. Part of what makes sudden singleness so difficult, especially for older women, is the way in which they spent their whole married lives defining themselves in terms of others. Even as children, we practice our current boyfriend's name prefixed by "Mrs.," playing with the idea of being his Missus. Late-in-life widowhood or divorce "doesn't have to mean being isolated, scared, poor, sick, sad, or stuck in old habits, attitudes, or feelings. Being alone doesn't have to mean being lonely. It can be a means of becoming an individual!"†

I'm more aware, now, of my own mortality; aware that my time is, if I'm lucky, not too long. It's not that I don't like this life, but I can't envision a long time of inactivity. I don't want to get into a state of vegetating. Of course, if I could be like George Abbott, who is nearly one hundred and is directing a new show . . . But my memory begins to taunt me with its absence and inaccuracies, and my agility is waning. I believe, and accept, that time is finite; and that makes me feel wonderful. I have made all my plans for the future and have no concerns. It's a lovely state of affairs for me and I hug every day to my heart.

Without realizing it, my mother gave me a great blessing, that of dependency—hers, on me. I was always a caretaker, starting at the age of six or seven. A sense of responsibility was part of me from the very beginning. At this stage of life, I am happier with myself than when I was very young. I even feel more attractive. My best weapon against possible moroseness is my curiosity. I want to know. I mean to take it all in while I can. I am tremendously interested in my contemporaries, how they are accepted and treated by the community. I am always ready to do battle for improved conditions. I don't seem to be able to tune out, to give up, to ignore. I dream of lying down, but I bless each morning for the variety of reasons I have for getting up.

---

* *Survival Handbook for Widows (and for relatives and friends who want to understand)*, Ruth Jean Loewinsohn, AARP Scott, Foresman & Co., Glenview, Ill., 1984
† *Alone—Not Lonely*, Jane Seskin, AARP Scott, Foresman & Co., Glenview, Ill., 1985

That Smaller World

I'm in the entertainment business—have been since I was five years old. You may not expect this of me, but I sound a note of warning: There's too much entertainment in our lives! Oh, I don't mean we should work harder and deny ourselves pleasure. Very much to the contrary. We must, somehow, learn again to create our own amusements. But more than that, we should accept that not every waking moment has to be fun. There seems to be a new psychological malaise: pleasure pressure. If I'm not having a high time, I must be missing something! Unfortunately, to most people that means being entertained by others, by professionals—athletes, actors, humorists, dancers, storytellers, celebrities. We buy divertissements and surround ourselves with gadgets, which are programmed to liven things up, day and night. A vast majority appears to be on a nonstop pleasure hunt.

The patron in the hotel lounge who asked that the TV be turned louder has no regard for others who were talking, laughing, and being pleased with each other's company. But more than that, when his friends came to join him, they exchanged a few words and then stared at the green screen together. This illustrates what goes on under the guise of togetherness and conviviality. We used to call family rooms "rumpus rooms." Are there still ping-pong tables taking up most of the space? So mundane an activity as eating bread may not rate as stimulating dinner conversation, unless it was homebaked; then it qualifies for "having a good time." The sudden, meteoric splash of the party game Trivial Pursuit indicates a national hunger for fun and games—of the self-induced variety. Pleasure pressure has been building. Letting off steam is difficult in the confines of an armchair.

Actors and actresses depend on the audience to surround the performance. Part of the method of rounding out the material is the reaction coming from across the footlights— be it silence, laughter, anguish, shock, embarrassment. That interaction is also part of what spectators give each other. Even a theater patron who comes unaccompanied to watch a play or a movie somehow becomes part of a brotherhood of spectators for the duration of the entertainment. Live theater is a shared, emotional adventure between audience and performers. This is emphatically shown by the new passion for standing ovations. People delight in taking part in the experience in that way. The Moiseyev dancers from the Soviet Union end their performance by applauding the audience.

Now comes a new type of audience: isolated loners. Singly, or in pairs, these folks focus on entertainment—a few inches beyond their two big toes—reclining, partially or fully, among pillows. Let's not go out this Saturday. We'll get a pizza and rent a couple of movies. The videocassette recorder plays to order for a few dollars a shot. No standing in line. No parking hassles. No baby-sitter. No costly dinner. But there is something missing. The audience. No film or play was ever written, directed, or acted for an audience of one. And most of them not for that minuscule stage, the TV screen. Comedy depends on the ripple effect of laughter to build to hilarity. Few of us will giggle or guffaw alone in a room with only a green flicker coming from a box. Horror, fear, shame, passion, compassion—every emotion is stronger in the presence of others watching the same scene. Fun is contagious. So is terror. I don't believe anyone has ever screamed hysterically while a cassette is unwinding. One million VCR units are sold every month, each to enthusiastic crowds of one or two. How many clap their hands at the end of the performance? For that matter, are they still awake?

"Of course I hardly ever watch TV, but did you happen to see what Linda Evans was wearing last night?" If you ask people, no one ever watches. Advertisers who get their information about TV viewers from Nielsen's poll get quite a different answer. Not only are "sets in use" multiplying, but through VCRs, each "set in use" is doubling in spades: We can record one channel and watch another. The problem is when to watch what one has taped. According to one estimate, only twenty percent of what is home-recorded is ever viewed. VCR owners build a personal library of taped sports and entertainment to bring out at some later date. Collecting stacks of unwatched shows gives a sense of relief to those who feel that life is passing them by. VCR owners feel duty-bound to snare and hold, perhaps for posterity. Is that what's called a sense of history?

There is an intriguing way to cheat when you own a VCR. You can watch sitcom junk and tape the cultural channel. When your friends talk about the great performances, you can always complain about your busy schedule and praise the wonders of delayed viewing. What psychological trauma may be engendered by eventually erasing a treasured tape has yet to be determined. Do you reuse the tape of last year's election, or the one where your uncle stood at the edge of a crowd during a street interview? Advertisers fear zapping—eliminating, erasing, or going fast forward during commercials. They should not worry. The hand on the button is not nearly as fast as eye and ear. Subliminal messages are held fast in the minds of the zappers—no matter how much they may try to avoid it. Once you own a VCR, you can, of course, forget about the dross that is available, free, on TV, and rent golden oldies. But you will discover that your tastes have changed over the years. And that is exactly why recording current programs is a waste of time and tape.

Those of us with long theatrical memories fear that this most expressive of all art forms may be pricing itself out of business. The best, most involved audiences have always been young theatergoers, whose enthusiasm and compelling interest in the theater is so unmistakably transmitted across the footlights to the performers. These people are no longer there. They cannot afford a hundred-dollar outing. Young families cannot bring their children and give them that first, wonderful exposure to the stage. Can teachers still bus the whole English class to learn about live performances?

The exorbitant costs of production occasionally gives way to one-man shows, a most rewarding form of theater. It's like having a story read to you by a favorite grown-up. So much is left for us, the audience to do—to think—to imagine. There is less distraction. One concentrates fully on a single actor. That performer shines even brighter when not burdened with the shortcomings of other actors. Only a superior talent will take on such a task and presume to have what it takes to carry off the whole show single-handedly. Brenda Currin, performer and adapter of an anthology by Eudora Welty, is such a talent. Her theatrical presentation *Sister and Miss Lexie* is a dramatic, entertaining tribute to one of America's most honored writers.

Miss Currin performs as though the words were spelled out in musical notes, with sharps and flats. She conducts with gestures, footsteps, and the tossing of her short blond hair. What she does with her voice, pursed lips, and widened, then narrowed eyes is pure mastery. She plays all the parts of a family of Southern ladies and their men folk, making them fully visible to the amused audience. Superb fiction adapted ingeniously to monodrama. "It's storytelling raised to dramatic art."

Broadway has venerable competition: New York's free theater, not only in parks and grandstands, but in some of the city's finest edifices. Raul Julia was heard, reading from his favorite authors, on the altar of St. Bartholomew's Church on Park Avenue. In that most beautiful Roman-esque-Byzantine cathedral gathered six or seven hundred people during lunch hour to hear readings from Tolstoy and Shakespeare. The acoustics of that structure, the reso-nant voice of Raul Julia, the truths of great minds—what cultural nourishment! The sounds of the city were inaudi-ble, but every whisper could be heard inside. One had to think that the Sermon on the Mount was not televised, amplified, taped, or recorded—yet everyone has heard it. The Ten Commandments were not Xeroxed, to be distrib-uted as handbills, but they have been memorized. Great truths, as well as simple wisdoms, are passed on by word of mouth. Free Theater Productions is bringing this back to lucky New Yorkers. The audience at St. Bart's was mostly women. I don't know why. Raul Julia was everyone's favor-ite cousin (or closer, yet) under that beautifully majestic ceiling.

Free theater is a boon, not only for the audience. Fine actors don't often have the opportunity to play the great roles or perform a favorite portion from literature, except in such a setting. In an audience, it reactivates, in some cases initiates, interest and enthusiasm in theater atten-dance and great literature for those who have lost or never had been in touch with inspiring arts. A most direct ap-proach to building audiences who will be attuned to the finest in stage acting, play writing, and literature.

Theatergoers stimulate each other to laugh. Televiewers have the laughter done for them by laugh tracks. When you consider the amount of uncensored frankness that spills out of prime-time television, you wonder why there's so much talk about censorship. What is left to be censored? Accord-ing to one source, which monitors textbooks, "no literature anthology published in the country today contains Shake-speare's *Romeo and Juliet* unexpurgated." Is Renaissance En-glish not fit for our eyes and ears? Was young love then more titillating than present-day soaps? Was there ever more gore and cruelty than in "crime-time" TV? Let us not tamper with the classics. Robert Linowes, head of the board of the Folger Shakespeare Library Theater, makes this provocative appraisal:

> We need classic theater not simply because it educates, enlightens, entertains, and not simply because it makes us laugh, weep, wonder, dream, believe and, sometimes, even suspend belief. We need a strong, vibrant classical theater because it is essential to our cultural well-being. Shakespeare, Molière, Chekhov, Ben Jonson—they embody the finest of our collective heritage. Thoreau once remarked, "What are the classics but the noblest recorded thoughts of man? They are the only oracles which are not decayed." Classical works are the best and most enduring of life's tragedies and comedies, by history's master stylists. Who hasn't been affected by the impotent confusion of Hamlet, the rage of Lear, the playfulness of Puck, the scheming of Iago, or the foolishness of Falstaff? How barren our culture would be without the drama of Shakespeare or Ibsen or Eugene O'Neill. In a culture increasingly anesthetized by television, where the average household watches more than six hours a day, the intellectual challenges of classical theater provide essential stimulation. In a society increasingly caught up in trivial pursuits, classical theater has the courage to take on universal themes. When "Dallas" is held up as the paragon of drama, when "Laverne and Shirley" is considered the height of comedy, when "The Gong Show" models human behavior, the value of classical theater is an essential antidote.

George Jean Nathan, the critic, thought of the theater as an escape from reality but also as a means to educate the emotions of the audience. Elia Kazan thinks of the theater as being dead now. Why? Because he is certain that theatergoers want to be shocked and there is nothing left that is still shocking. That is just absurd! Patrons of the arts want to be uplifted; they want to be moved, amused, stimulated, and made to think. They want to be stirred and, yes, perhaps the more immature want to be shocked. If the top brass thinks like Kazan, then that is why theater is sick.

Of course, all this comes down to one's concept of the theater, and I think I learned from some of the great actors and actresses to whom I was exposed that the theater is an instrument of civilization, a means to educate the human soul. Theater is memorable—a durable instrument. People tell me how they remember being taken as a child to see me in *Victoria Regina*, or that attending a play was part of their honeymoon—and that theater became part of their lives. I cherish my stage idols the same way. Laurette Taylor. I went again and again to see her perform her magic. She never made an exit; she just walked away. When she paid *me* the compliment of asking for my autographed picture I begged for a swap of photos. I sent mine, inscribed "To my Guiding Star." Hers came in that day's mail: "To Helen, who knew how to follow her star." I went for weeks and weeks to see Mrs. Minnie Maddern Fiske, that great comedienne and interpreter of intellectual drama. (My matinees were Wednesday; hers were Thursday.) What I hoped to understand was her seemingly spontaneous technique. What I learned was that she managed to make every move, every inflection, even flicking a crumb off the table accurately the same day after day.

Tyrone Guthrie of London and Minnesota said, "I believe that a theater where live actors perform to an audience which is there in the flesh before them will survive all threats from powerfully organized industries which pump prefabricated drama out of cans and blowers and contraptions of one kind or another. The struggle for survival will often be hard and will batter the old theater about severely. Indeed from time to time it will hardly be recognizable—but it will survive. It will survive as long as mankind demands to be amused, terrified, instructed, shocked, corrupted, and delighted by tales told in the manner which will always remain mankind's most vivid and powerful manner of telling a story."

Oh, Oh,
Here We Go Again

In the days of the famed Algonquin round table, Charles MacArthur and I made every effort to be last to leave. It was Charlie's contention that one must, at all cost, avoid leaving two others to talk about you . . . just what *we* did, all the way home to Nyack. What funny stories shine like jewels in that mosaic of memory! These tiny tiles make up the picture of a life. They enchant me now when I remember so many of these unrelated experiences, especially the best-foot-backwards kind of happenings.

I love to dwell on things people have said to me, strangers who come on with, what will be, their "most embarrassing" story. Of course, there are annoyances, but now and then I get rewarded.

What has always amazed me is my astounding hold on the public, which is not based on acting marvels, I'm sure. Half of those who come up to me and say, "I have to hug you—I have to kiss you" have probably never seen me on the stage. Maybe they saw me in one or two pictures in which I certainly wasn't any good. But I think I have come to understand it; it is that I am so totally average. My image is somewhat blurred and thus can fit anyone's need. You couldn't push Marlene Dietrich into some vacant spot in your life. Nor Garbo, nor Joan Collins. Not only do I seem to mirror hundreds of mothers, wives, aunts, and beloved grannies, I am also often mistaken for other people. When Nelson Rockefeller was vying for the presidential nomination on the Republican ticket, he invited me to Miami to stand with him and Happy in a reception line for the delegates. So I went. There was Kitty Carlisle Hart, Hildegarde, and a few other stars of stage and television—those few Republicans who happen to be in my business. As I have come to expect, I was paid more than a fair share of attention. But what people were saying to me were such things as "Oh, I remember you so well in *The Barretts of Wimpole Street.* I saw you when you played in Detroit in *Medea;* you were superb." Oh, they had me doing the most unlikely parts! This happens to me so often that I have learned not to argue. I just accept it with gracious thanks. At the end, Hildegarde said to me: "Well, my dear, you were the star of the evening." And I told her: "You're mistaken; I was three stars—Kate Cornell, Judith Anderson, and also Mary Martin once or twice. And, oh yes, Lillian Gish, of course."

Lillian and I seem to transmigrate into each other all the time. I went to the island of Mykonos in Greece—years ago, before Mykonos became a jet-set focal point. There was only one hotel—a charming little family-run place. And as we entered the lobby, there stood the full-bosomed proprietess with her arms outstretched, ready to enfold me with Greek ardor: "Oh, I love you. I love you. You have changed my life." And then she explained that when she was carrying her baby she prayed that if it were a girl, she would be like she remembered me in *Broken Blossoms.* And, she assured me, the girl grew up to be just like me, all because I supposedly cast this wonderful spell over her and her baby. For the remainder of our stay I entered and exited by the rear door to avoid the dear lady. I thought it would destroy her if she suddenly woke up to the fact that she had me confused with Lillian Gish.

It seems that my great attraction for the public, the reason I have held this place in the hearts of the people, is that I *am* average and that I'm not a distant, awesome star, but cozy and close at hand. They feel I belong to them.

During the run of *Harriet*, I traveled to the theater by bus. It was wartime and gas was rationed, and although I could have gotten supplementary allowances, I felt duty-bound (and noble) to conserve for the war effort. It was a big scramble for the last bus from New York. It was always packed; many stood all the way. One time a man and his wife seemed to be talking about me, she obviously urging him to speak to me. Finally, she gave him a nudge and he made his way to me through the crowd. When he reached my side, he said "Miss Hayes, my wife wants me to tell you that if this bus is good enough for us, it's good enough for Helen Hayes." I managed to thank him most cordially, without even cracking a smile. I'm sure he woke up in the middle of the night with, "My God, what did I say!"

Into that category of best-meant wishes of flustered men falls this little vignette. A store clerk, an elderly man, is enraptured by a little blond moppet of two or so. He bends to her level for a few minutes while the doting young mother looks on. In parting, the smitten man looks up at the woman and says, "You must have a very handsome husband."

My grandson Charlie managed such a gaffe when he dined at the White House, seated next to Secretary Donald Regan's lovely daughter. "How's the food here?" he wanted to know before putting the fork (foot?) in his mouth.

That same day brings to mind a number of Oh! No! kind of stories. It was just before the Statue of Liberty centennial celebration. President Reagan mentioned to me that no one had told him yet what his function would be. And little Helen big-mouth speaks up: "I can tell you; I heard it from the horse's mouth, David Wolper. You will first light the blue laser beam and then light the torch slowly . . ." etc., etc. I probably caused a minor security shakeup. Maybe this is why I was bumped from a flight to Crested Butte, Colorado, recently.

But the President has his own little yarn to remember that day. Seven of us were to be awarded the Freedom Medal. I was the only woman (and by the way, the only one who walked without a cane). To share my great honor with my late husband, I had requested that the citation should be to Helen Hayes MacArthur. When my turn came to be called by the President, he said, "Helen Hayes," and I looked disappointedly at Nancy Reagan, whose nod tried to reassure me. I started to my feet, prepared to jump up the steps, and our Chief of State said, "Not now, Helen, sit down." He was first going to tell the story about Charlie and the emeralds and peanuts. (And if you don't know it, you have missed it about five thousand times.)

One of the most repeated experiences of my life are the fans who just stare at me and eventually decide to ask if anyone has ever told me that I resemble Helen Hayes. My standard answer: "All my life." Sometimes that satisfies them. But the lady in Crested Butte, Colorado, who followed me along a sparkling trout stream persisted: "Well you do. You really do." At that point, there is nothing left than to deflate the hot-air balloon with a deft and pointed "I am!"

Fame has its price and its rewards. One afternoon, I shook four hundred hands, standing all the while at a reception for volunteers for Mothers' March of Dimes. Then I saw this lovely little creature coming up to me. Very elderly, with a white fringe of bangs under a little pillbox hat with flowers, a white jabot at her neck, a dainty, delicate apparition. I couldn't let her go by with just my nod and tired smile. I said warmly, "Thank you so much for helping us." And she answered, "I can't claim to have helped. I just came because I wanted to meet you. My special interest is sex deviation."

Once I had a neighbor named Alexandra Tolstoy, who was the daughter of the great Leo Tolstoy. We became good friends, after having been introduced by Anton Dolin, the famous choreographer. Many a Sunday summer afternoon I sat on her porch, sampling the Russian delicacies she spread out around the samovar. When the time came for the world to celebrate the centennial of Leo Tolstoy's birth, I received a frantic call from Alexandra: We had to do something—to plan an event. She was very put out by the French Academy of Arts and Letters, who had commissioned all the top writers of the day to write and rhyme tributes to the master—all without consulting or including her. In England the same thing had happened. Now, she wanted to do the American tribute to her father, with me. Since I heartily doubted that I was right for this assignment, I offered to put her in touch with someone like John Steinbeck or my close friend Thornton Wilder, who I knew would round up a wonderful group of artistic people. Well, she jumped on me! "I don't want any of your so-called writers of America. I must do this for my father—alone. It must have dignity." She was a terrifyingly strong-willed woman.

Finally, she worked out her program. She hired Town Hall. All the Tolstoys were to attend, and other White Russian émigrés would be in the audience. The program consisted of a piano recital, children dancing in country costumes, and then she read an endless, favorite passage from Tolstoy's works—in her low, slow, heavily accented speech. One couldn't understand much of it. Then I went on to read another passage. And that was all; that was the program. I had visions of negative press coverage by some indignant critics, which could easily have drummed me out of the theater in New York. I prayed to God to save me from the dire effects of this misadventure. (I was playing in *Happy Birthday*, by Anita Loos, at the time—quite a jump, as you can imagine.) And God did intervene. The producer of our extravaganza had overlooked one little detail—she had neglected to publicize it. There wasn't a word about it anywhere. No one came but a few Tolstoys and émigrés—and Irish me. And, so, we did the whole thing in secret.

It is usually quite hopeless for me to try and put on airs of loftiness, to put on the grand act. When we were rehearsing *Arrowsmith* all those many years ago, the great director John Ford was getting somewhat restless and strained. He had made a promise to "stay on the wagon" until the picture was finished; failure to do so threatened instant replacement. His irritability was usually calmed by my presence; he adored me and we always had a wonderful relationship. He was known to follow me around, even to other cities when I played there. He was cutting away at a scene, slashing lines that were rather important between Ronald Colman and me; we ended up with no more than a couple of broken phrases. So I said: "Oh, Jack, you're not going to be able to get away with this. Sam Goldwyn will just make us do it all over again." There was a moment's pause and then he said in clipped tones: "I am the director, directing this picture. *You* are performing in it. I tell *you* what to do and *you* do what I tell you. And that is all *you* are expected to do." Well, I tottered to my little chair that had "Helen Hayes" blazoned on it and flopped into it. Deathly silence reigned all over the set—from behind scenery to the highest parallels where the light crew dangled. Everybody had heard this. Finally, Ford came over to me, chewing on the corner of his habitual handkerchief. "What's the matter, honey, did I make ya mad?" I answered loud and clear and with great dignity: "I am not accustomed to being *speaken* to in that tone!" That was the best laugh I have ever gotten in my whole career of comedy.

Periodically, I have bouts with hoof-in-mouth disease. I had an invitation to meet Mother Teresa at Catholic University in Washington. It meant the world to me to have the opportunity to be in the presence of a saint. I was not planning to do more than stand there, but someone insisted on dragging me into the inner circle where she sat, surrounded by her disciples in their blue-bordered white saris. She was playing with a little child of two or three, who was so enraptured by this woman. They had this great rapport. An aura of love filled the room. I stood there, planning what I could say to so special a being. But, when we shook hands, Mother Teresa said, verbatim, what I had rehearsed: "You do so much good; God must love you." I was upstaged, but it took a saint to do it.

An even loftier religious experience was with Pope John

Paul. My friend Lari Mako wanted desperately to be granted
a private audience, as had Dolores Hope and Irène Dunne,
her mentors. We prevailed on Cardinal Cooke to arrange it
and then flew together from London to Rome, just for the
day. She insisted on dressing in an ankle-length black gown
and lace mantilla. But, as we were advised not to wear all
black, she added a fair quantity of fine jewelry. I, quite
obediently, also wore black. When we arrived at the Vatican,
there were twenty thousand other faithful in the crowded
square. The Pope was sequestered behind a wide circle of
wooden sawhorses, seated on the papal throne in the center. The people formed a sea of colorful dresses, T-shirts,
denim, and madras. We could hardly have been more conspicuous as we were led across the empty circle to take our
place on the other side, to wait our turn. I was thoroughly
embarrassed. First, he made his circle around the barrier,
blessing the people. And as he approached us, I was the first
to greet him and kiss the ring. He suddenly looked up, way
up above the crowd, and took his hand away to wave to
some nuns in the distance. He then started to leave. I pan-
icked because I saw that the photographer had not reached
us yet. Poor Lari, she would be crushed. And then I did the
unthinkable. I clutched the Pope, I grabbed him. He looked
absolutely horrified. Suddenly, I was more devoted to my
friend than any higher power. She had to have her picture.
She now possesses a lovely photo of serenity to commemo-
rate the occasion. Mine, on the other hand, is one of a man
staring down at me in disbelief.

Work Ethic—
an Oxymoron

Work is wonderful. Work is awful. Ethically, it is thoroughly contradictory. I hasten to explain that oxymoron is not a hard worker, dumb as an ox. The word defines itself by not meaning what it sounds like.

Attitudes about work undergo constant changes. Until recently, compensation for working was "dough"; now it is "bread." This may illustrate a lack of patience: we have not got time to wait for the former to turn into the latter.

"Despite economic recovery, America's labor market seems to have shut down for young people. While total national unemployment hovers near 7%, youth joblessness stands at 16% for whites, 24% for Hispanics, and 43% for blacks."* The underlying reasons are many. Technology eliminates many entry-level jobs. Soaring manufacturing costs drive industries out of densely populated cities, where the labor force is concentrated. Some industries leave the country for tax or labor reasons. Without ever having had entry-level jobs, young people cannot develop skills and appropriate workplace attitudes. In other western industrialized nations, such as France, it is the twentieth century there, too. But there one can feel the pride young people take in doing their jobs well. Without that sense of pride, one cannot develop respect for society and for self. Working, and getting paid, is important during the years when young people "sort out their identities and build lifetime principles."† Unfortunately, Congress vetoed the creation of an American Conservation Corps. Instead of caring for our national parks, potential conservationists express their frustration by scribbling unintelligible messages on walls, trucks, and trains. The French countryside sprouts flowers, not soda cans, broken railings, missing guideposts, or spray-can murals. Villages and city sidewalks are washed in the early morning and swept—never into the gutter. Who does these jobs? Old people, young people, working together. We do have some excellent projects run by cities, states, and industry. But not nearly enough! Community service is just one aspect. Industry *must* make room for young people.

It is only natural to try to protect our children from hardships and deprivations that we may have experienced. In a country such as ours, where so many are the product of immigration or are the first generation, we tend to strive for the good life. Nothing wrong with that. Most of us know we have to work for it. Old-timers revere work. Are children allowed to learn that, still? We are so gadget-geared that youngsters have a tough time discovering that there is duty as well as pleasure and that these concepts are not mutually exclusive. What is fun? And what gives satisfaction? How to achieve personal enjoyment? Ask that question of adults and children and you will get a variety of answers, more often than not based on entertainment and on activities involving others. A show. Concerts. Friends. Eating out. Buying things. Travel. Free time. The weather. What about a job well done? A mundane chore? A challenging task?

Satisfaction derived from having done what was once called duty is an almost alien concept to children today. They may get pleasure from their ritual hair shampooing and blow-drying, but not the weekly laundry. They may spend the better part of the weekend prowling the stores for a new-wave item, but they won't happily do the week's marketing. If there is no satisfaction in doing chores, it may become more and more difficult to determine just what is fun. A pet is fun. Caring for it is not. Books that tell parents how to amuse their children on a rainy day or during summer vacation never say paint a room, build a doghouse, rent a rug shampooer to wash the carpets, barefoot. Plant an herb garden. Repair old toys to bring to the sick or the poor. A youngster who learns that work and even duty can be fun is less likely to have to go far—and, eventually, too far—to find it.

When the alarm clock performs its preset function, no doubt you respond with preprogrammed dismay. You may not actually throw it across the room; nonetheless, you have no kind words for it, such as "Thank you for announcing a new dawn; I would hate to have missed it." Or, "What a treat! A whole, bright day, all mine!" You think I am joking. Your head is under the pillow to stifle a curse. Well, not if you know what's good for you. Your job is, if you have one. Paid employment has a positive effect on psychological well-being. Why do we automatically resent facing a new day? We are conditioned to complain about work, bosses, employees, co-workers, and traffic. In fact, regular, daily employment has distinct health benefits, directly attributable to self-satisfaction. Performance and efficiency on the job carry over into private life.

Relationships with co-workers, however imperfect they may be, are important and are different from those one has at home. They offer a reprieve from the often emotionally "high charged" relationships with people close to us. Less overt criticism. Easier rapport. Fewer finicky demands. More self-control. Small talk and office gossip relieve tensions created by weighty matters that surround us. One of the job-related boosts to psychological wellness is teamwork. Contact with others is stimulating; it gives encouragement and feedback. Most of what overwhelms us at home is the feeling of having to "do it all": "Everything's up to me." "I never get any help . . ." Outside the home, we usually work with others, who assume part of the responsibility but also share in the success or failure. Being a part of the whole creates a feeling of strength and the pleasure of cooperation. A job offers a personal point of reference; what we *do* is who we are.

Having a schedule by which to live may not be drudgery at all. In fact, it promotes a sense of security and purpose. One tradition that seems to withstand the test of time (and that I find amazing), is the nine-to-five, Monday-through-Friday work schedule. Why should that be, when the needs of the workplace have changed so much and science allows for day and night to be equalized? Food is grown under artificial conditions and harvested mechanically. Transportation has no season or hours. Weather is rarely a factor. Family life manages to survive without most old traditions: who works, who nurtures, who's too young or too old—for *anything.*

Alternative work schedules exist, of course, but are not yet available on a large enough scale. Not being a social scientist, I am not quite sure where it must start. Let's try the schools, first. If working mothers could choose when their children go to school and when their vacations are, wouldn't that facilitate the rearing of children by those who want to and should be doing it? Children go to school from eight to three, with several free hours in between; there are over forty weekends and frequent vacations. School facilities and staff are underutilized at least a third of the time. Working parents try to cope with a schedule that is simply unworkable. Why not flextime, in school *and* on the job? Alternative labor schedules benefit the operation of companies. Productivity increases, family relations improve, employment can become possible throughout the ever-lengthening life span. Machines can produce without humans. But we need work to feel productive. Besides flexible scheduling and part-time employment, there are other alternatives for optimal utilization of human resources—job sharing, job rotation, phased retirement, second and third careers, and two and three shifts. I hope we will not have to put every metropolis under a dome before we learn to utilize *all* our resources—man, moment, and matter—to the best advantage.

"Room at the top" encourages us to strive for forward motion in work, art, politics, or whatever engages our time. It is actually a very apt description of the zenith in any given field. There is plenty of space up there because so few make it and many of those who do do not stay very long. There is a lack of applicants for top positions. Many ambitious people who spend a lifetime climbing make an unexpected halt just before their goal. Was it lack of ability? It may have more to do with fear of success. Apparently, even those who drive themselves toward the apex of their profession falter just before they reach the winner's circle, not for lack of talent or aspiration, but because other psychological factors deter them. Sometimes, "people promoted in the morning are hospitalized in the afternoon."‡

Not every conscious effort to succeed is actually intended to do so. Some strivers are said to sabotage their own road to glory, however subtly they may go about it. Why does the author hesitate to submit the manuscript, which is ready and has been accepted? Perhaps the specter of the critics is too overwhelming. Why does the executive refuse to step up the ladder? It may be that greater exposure is too intimidating. Outside of commerce or the arts, in social positions, success can also create problems—real or imagined. Friends or relatives may resent your aiming higher than they do. Tribal traditions, such as knocking on wood; saying "break a leg!"; or spitting over the shoulder prevent us from overreaching our grasp at the moment of impending success. Fear of jealous gods or envious peers makes us shrink from the imagined dangers of success. The trick is to understand that such roadblocks are self-fabricated.

Biographical sketches of artists, writers, and composers always include material about their work habits. Where does the creative output get transferred to paper or onto canvas? In the proverbial garret? Locked in a study or studio at the far end of the house? In a separate, little house?

And which part of the day is set aside for inspired creativity? From sunup till noon? Or not until later in the day? In short, everyone who works at home must keep to a strict set of self-imposed rules. Unless one learns to distinguish between work and home, working at home is *not* going to work. Especially for a woman. She must make constant decisions: Press her advantage in a business deal, or do the shirts? Cook up a new scheme for a client or a batch of applesauce? Balance the business bookkeeping or the family checkbook? Obviously, there is need for discipline, be it in art, industry, medicine, or management.

One of the side effects of working at home is that you now lack a place to come home to for relaxation. Once you associate your dwelling with business, it is no longer for the sake of living there that you are working. On the other hand, working at home puts you in control. Your time is your own. You can switch on the message machine and go to play golf. Getting down to serious work at home requires motivation, dedication, and feeling comfortable with isolation.

Part-timers and "office temps" have become an important part of the economy. Such workers used to be considered more or less unskilled, even unreliable, and given low-paying, uninteresting jobs. All this has changed. Companies now see the wisdom of augmenting their staff during peak seasons. Workers appreciate the flexibility of working on their own schedules in a variety of occupations. And employment agencies have discovered a whole new market: a new pool of employable people. The first thought that comes to mind is that part-timers do not get fringe benefits, such as health insurance. But even that is changing, since some of these specialized employment agencies now offer health benefits after a specified period of employment through their services. Businesses that hire such workers are surprised to find increased productivity. The Department of Labor estimates that temps are engaged in work 90% of the time they are on the job, compared with 65% to 80% performance by permanent employees.

If you phone a business office and a man answers, "Mr.

Redwood's office," you may well think it's Mr. Redwood himself and begin your conversation. If you are lying in a hospital bed and a man in white coat, stethoscope in hand, asks you "how you doin'?" you'll think it's time to tell your troubles to this intern. But in fact, the first man is a secretary and the second a nurse—not a nurse waiting to be a doctor, but a nurse by choice. Not enough men choose professions that traditionally have been occupied by women. Of course, some do. In 1960, there were just over 14,000 male registered nurses; in 1980, close to four times as many, while the number of women nurses only doubled. But in the secretarial field, only about 7,000 more men took such a job in that twenty-year period, while an additional 1 1/2 million women joined the ranks.

The best marriages are those where both husband and wife have interests and responsibilities once considered feminine. Oh, I can see macho types cringe and *real* women gasp at the thought. But it may well be true. To enjoy life and have an interest in all manner of things almost dictates that among them will be traditionally feminine pursuits. Men who reject much of what occupies a woman's mind and her time have to withdraw from all those activities and resort to what is left—the masculine endeavors: job, politics, sports. The German phrase that separates the men from a big chunk of the real world is "Kinder, Kirche, Küche," which defines the woman's role as "children, church, kitchen." In my view, those interests, and their variations and side effects, are the mainstay of life. Men who exclude themselves are the poorer for it.

Men still do not have an easy time in the workplace, dealing with women who occupy other than the traditional roles. "Men can get into the habit of dealing with autonomous women only if they experienced it at home."** Those who had the advantage of growing up in the company of a sister, for example, may have a better start in recognizing women as separate persons. As yet, women do not really belong to themselves. Just think of the traditional wedding ceremony, in which the bride is "given away" by her father.

Are there still dowries, those antiquated payoffs to the groom and his family? These "family politics" have their counterpart in commerce. Just as children are the last available inferiors within the family structure, women are still subjected to wage discrimination in the workplace.

"Overall, 'women's work' pays about $4,000 less annually than does 'men's work.' In fact, the average male high-school dropout earns more than the average female college graduate. In one recent court case, a judge maintained the right of the City of Denver to continue paying hospital nurses less than maintenance workers and tree trimmers because the comparable worth principle was (in his words), 'pregnant with the possibility of disrupting the entire economic system of the United States.' "†† Merely admitting that paying women more would disrupt our economy is a sign of blatant discrimination. Taking into account different skills, which may involve strength versus dexterity, leadership versus nurturing, pay equity measures the quality of male and female work and reflects the *real* work value.

Now and then, one reads of renewed attempts at giving unsalaried housework and family management equal status with "real" work. Nothing ever comes of it. We are given conflicting signals about what *is* work, what should occupy us, what are honorable ways to fill our days. In return, we send garbled information about our activities.

I'm so glad you found a few moments to relax with a book. At least I hope you did, and aren't doing three other things at the same time. I know how busy you are. Everyone is, these days. Have you noticed? Children don't play anymore; they *work* out or *work* their computers. Women don't go to lunch just to chat with a friend for an hour. They "grab" a bite on the way to or from. When was the last time you had company on Sunday afternoon for purely social purposes, not for an event, banquet, fund-raising, meeting, or networking? Busy people don't talk about how busy they are. I have a friend who will tell me at length how much time it takes to care for her houseplants. Now really! Free-lancers, in any field, are expert at making their lives sound like the cabin scene in *Night at the Opera* when, in fact, they are technically unemployed. Sometimes, it seems guilt under- lies the national mania to project an air of busyness. (Some- one is sitting in front of all those TV screens, hours on end! Or are pollsters fabricating their findings?) The other major mania is shopping, not to be equated with buying, mind you. A lot of talk about how busy one is, is just that: talk. Idleness, it is drummed into us, is sinful. To that we have added the modern interpretation of productiveness: it must produce income or perspiration. But even volunteer work, commendable as it is, is often based on involving a maxi- mum number of people in a task that could be done better by one dedicated worker. Work is a fine remedy against many ills. Faking it is to the contrary.

I overheard a conversation between two young women: "Well, I really do think he is more of a generalist, a humanist actually; I see him as a scientist, perhaps." Turns out they were discussing their children—school children! Across the room, there were the usual discussions about where to find a competent plumber, that electricians are charging more than psychiatrists, and whether carpenters still know how to wield hammers or only automatic stapling guns. This social chitchat brings into sharp focus a little argument going on in suburbia: What happens to property value when trades- people buy homes in these prissy enclaves and proceed to park panel trucks or vans in their driveways? Frankly, what I think happens is a healthier interweaving of society. Blue- and white-collar workers will be less likely to mistrust each other.

Our society was not always so divisive. Teachers and preachers who traveled across the plains together with herders and cartwrights did not park their wagons in sepa- rate circles at night. "Translate" the names of famous Americans and high society back to their actual meanings and you will find "Ford," who perhaps ran the river ferry; and "Cartwright," who made wheels; "Smith," "Taylor," and "Koch"—all good folks with talented hands. That young mother who projected her own biases onto her child's future refuses to entertain the notion that he might want to fix motors, build roofs, or raise chickens. Why not? Perhaps because our upwardly mobile mentality does not allow for a panel truck in the neighbor's driveway to advertise the profession of its owner. A doctor's brass shingle, O.K. A piano teacher's name plate, acceptable. What happened to good old American egalitarian red, white, and blue?

* Franklin Thomas, President, Ford Foundation
† Ibid.
‡ Dr. Jesse Cavenar, Professor of Psychiatry, Duke University
** *Family Politics: Love and Power on an Intimate Frontier*, Letty Cottin Pogrebin, McGraw-Hill, New York, 1983
†† Jean Robinson, Professor and Chairman/Consumer Economics and Housing, Cornell University

Money Makes
the World Go 'Round

After the second war, as part of a theater group, I toured the South Pacific for the State Department. One of our stops was the Philippine islands, where we spent a month. I was quartered in a convent, and through its mother superior (a most charming woman), I was introduced to the Marcos family. She took me to the palace one afternoon to meet them and to sightsee. But that is a long time ago. It was not all gussied up then. You might say I knew the Marcoses when they were poor. Since then, they have become a unique aberration on a multitude of levels, not the least of which is the zenith of conspicuous consumption.

The truth of numbers and the value of money are losing all meaning. Thus, my pavane for the penny. That shiny copper disk no longer has a reason for being. Look at it. Abraham Lincoln is there to reaffirm that "In God We Trust"; the Treasury Building represents freedom from want. The penny proclaims the most compelling word for *E Pluribus Unum:* Liberty. And yet, it has no status. Children will no longer bend to pick it up, thank you for it, hoard it, or prize it (unless it's from 1849).

Baby talk for a number with a hundred zeros is "googol."

It is in the dictionary, right after "goofy," and is, in fact, used by mathematicians who worry that the national debt may reach this number. They are trying to contain it at a mere 1.5 trillion. I did not know how many zeros that takes until I saw it in the paper: only eleven.

Government is supposed to represent a sort of father figure. Watching its fiscal fandango hardly inspires good, old-time prudence in personal finance. Inflation, in its simplest terms, means that no price tag is too high because very soon it will be higher. One does not have to be an economist to be concerned. Congress, in charge of keeping hold of the federal purse strings, has had to relax its "predetermined" grip seventy-five times in sixty-five years. So, how can we learn or remember the true significance of money? I can stand outside a bank and have tens and twenties pop out of a slot in the wall by simply inserting a plastic card. If the machine "eats" the card by mistake, I am out of cash for the weekend. If it delivers ten dollars short, the bank manager will, grudgingly, believe me if I look more honest than his thieving machine, which reveals no record of shortchanging me. How do the poor in the street feel as I pull money toward me? And would a child bend down if I dropped some of it?

Everyone can afford a "designer" wardrobe, it seems, and even youngsters shop on credit. Who still understands money? When it was the child's duty to carry the milk can to the store with a few coins clutched in his hand, he learned the value of money early in life. If he dropped his pennies and they rolled into the sewer, he took the longest way home, knowing that retribution was inescapable. Grandmother says "a penny for your thoughts" to the little daydreamer, but I doubt her offer is still irresistible. No one plays penny-ante poker anymore. Pennies from heaven are not in the least welcome. Girl infants are not named Penelope, for fear the diminutive will be an insult. There are no penny arcades (it costs a quarter to play). Only one subject still gives the lowly copper coin a bit of polish: Gold is still measured in pennyweight. I do not know why.

The old gentleman, waiting for his wife to complete her purchase at a clothing store, observed a youngster who dropped a penny as she was leaving. "You dropped a penny, Miss," he said solicitously. She turned her pretty head to look at him, then at the red copper on the floor, and went out saying "I know." The man was speechless, for a while. Then, shaking his head, he told me how this angers him. Poor man; he cannot adjust to the change of values, although he knows that a penny buys nothing. He cannot cope with the rudeness either, I am sure. Could that youngster not have said, "Gee, thanks," and picked it up just to be polite? I wait for my two cents change on the $1.98 purchase, not because the coins matter, but because I feel I would insult the cashier if I walked away.

Children and money is a subject that is not taken seriously enough. In my time (as the saying goes), small ones were treated to a few coins, now and then, and encouraged to hoard them in a piggy bank. School children had to produce a budget for Dad to calculate a pared-to-the-bone allowance. Occasionally there would be a bonus—a quarter, or even a whole dollar, for a good report card. Children could earn spending money. (It was a lot less dangerous out there then!) In 1940, the going rate for baby-sitting was twenty-five cents an hour. There were paper routes and stockroom chores, leaf raking, snow shoveling, car washing. Caddying paid quite well; scraping barnacles off boat bottoms was arduous, but profitable. All of it was considered character building. *Earned* money is spent differently. Real money, laid down on the counter, makes more of an impact than a credit card.

Today's teenagers enjoy a false affluence. They are the target group on whom billions are spent by advertisers, and they respond according to projections. As a group, they spend $48 *billion* a year! Primarily on nonessentials. Early affluence, however, does not a wise consumer make. On the contrary, it may lead to trouble. Since most teens live at home or at school, the money they spend is considered discretionary. (It's not a synonym for "with discretion.")

Stereos, watches, cameras, televisions, computers, jewelry, makeup, cars, clothes. Once spending habits are formed, they are hard to break. Parents who shield their children from the family's financial facts of life think they are being protective. But consumer skills come from experience. Let teenagers take care of the family checkbook chores? Why not! It contains valuable lessons.

It does not take long to discover that money is a powerful, magical ego- and status-builder. We use it as a tool to suit our purpose. We promise a purchase or a cash reward for good behavior. We threaten to withhold it for childhood infractions. Children overhear talk of loss and gain. Even shady deals and tax evasion are sometimes discussed within their hearing. They see that we judge others by their wealth, or lack of it. So will they, pretty soon. It is little wonder, then, that most children fear poverty, admire wealth, and many try pilfering from mother's purse or dad's wallet to test themselves. They leave easy-to-follow trails of their petty crimes because, unconsciously, they want to be caught and stopped. It is at that point that the adult faces the delicate job of teaching, punishing, encouraging, explaining.

Children gauge not only others but themselves by how much money they have. Television is the tutor. They have seen and heard a great deal about the consequences of poverty, which to them holds the threat of abandonment. No wonder they try to build their own secret nest eggs, honestly or otherwise. If new ice skates are out of the question, but new tires are bought for the family car, the child needs an explanation of the difference between wants and needs. Grandparents play a major role in a child's perception of money. There is a tendency to "buy" love, to flaunt generosity, to counter what the parents stand for. Don't bring a gift every time. Don't buy what was denied as being too expensive, extravagant, or unwarranted. If you want to give cash gifts for special occasions, the child does not have to know about it.

Learning about money is becoming more and more difficult. Credit cards are part of the problem. They are phantom money. They enslave, rather than liberate. This bumper sticker explains the daily commute: "I owe. I owe. So off to work I go." Right after I have signed a credit slip, I am always a bit angry with myself. Not for having made a purchase, but for signing my name without checking the calculation. We try to remember that $12.98 is, in fact, $13.00. And that the sales tax adds another dollar. But what about interest? What interest? The interest on the charges you are racking up on your account. Do you know what percent interest your credit-card company charges? Twelve and a half percent? Seventeen percent? Eighteen and a half percent? Twenty-one point-six percent? The average interest rate on purchases not paid in full within the billing period is an incredible 18.6 percent. If your average outstanding balance throughout the year is a mere $500, you could be paying more than $100 in interest. That is more than one dollar out of every five, buying you nothing. Credit-card companies are in business to make money. But 132 percent profit!! Is that fair?

Paying cash or by check is the obvious way to avoid the additional cost of buying with plastic. Paying in full within the billing period is another. In the last four years, just about every interest rate charged in the United States has fallen, except on credit-card purchases. Find out just what you are paying in interest for the privilege of dawdling over your bills. If, on the other hand, you are quick to pay but once in a while leave a small balance, be careful not to add large amounts. The interest rate might apply not only to what you owed from last month, but to the new charges, too.

We all say it often enough: "I just don't know where the money goes." But that is not really true, except in the case of taxes. Wouldn't it be lovely if, on the last line of the tax form, we could specify how we want our contribution to the general good to be used. It has been said that tax investigators are more concerned with how we spend our money than how the government spends it. The government is on our payroll *and* gives the orders! As sure as irises bloom in the spring, so do IRS forms.

Have you ever asked yourself how families managed on one income for so long, when today's two-income, childless couples can barely scrape by? I do not think it is all to be blamed on inflation. After all, salaries are also climbing skyward. When one person stayed home to do what she considered her "job," the style of living was quite different. She made it her business to contribute, in her own way, by shopping with care, marketing with a plan, doing a lot of the maintenance and chores herself. When both householders work outside the home, eating in restaurants is part of the routine—often three times a day, each. Food purchases aim at convenience, rather than budget. Many services, including laundry, are done on the outside. Finances and investments are not always handled properly since there is so little free time. To compensate for the arduous hours of work, leisure pursuits become indulgences.

Young couples find it so difficult to buy their own homes, they try to soothe their frustrations with cars, vacations, club memberships, and the like. That money, of course, is gone, whereas the house their parents bought, many years ago, has multiplied in value far beyond expectation. I am glad to see a small ground swell of the old liberating American ethic, the do-it-yourself and take-me-as-I-am mentality, to counteract the image-building that has so many people by the purse strings. Rehabilitating old houses, pasta and wine dinners, garage sale mania, and flea market outings. It is again chic to "make your own"—from pot pies to paintings, antiques to argyles, bread and wine. If the young executive gets a $10,000 raise, it may occur to him or her to order matched crystal stemware in eight sizes from Tiffany's. But who is going to stand behind the dining room chair, with white cotton gloves, to pour the Rothschild Lafite? And who ends up doing the dishes?

"What, you make that much money and still don't have . . . ?" To become a professional financial planner takes little more than a trip to the print shop to order business cards and stationery. Plug in a telephone and presto! anyone can be a financial planner. Unlike other professions, there are presently little or no industrywide licensing or testing standards. There is no question that in these volatile financial times, everyone should have a personal or family financial plan. It is complicated to do it ourselves. Competent professional help can make a big difference in conserving and supplementing one's finances and give an accurate overview of earnings, expenditures, and how money should be saved and invested for the future. There are many legitimate financial planners to choose from. But please be aware that millions of dollars are siphoned off by some swindlers.

An unscrupulous financial planner, usually a self-proclaimed smooth talker, has only one interest: to put some of your money in his pockets. Therefore, it is imperative to scrutinize his background, credentials, business reputation, and track record. The key question to ask is not "How much money will you make for me?" If the percentage promised far exceeds the market average, be forewarned. Too good is not good. Ask instead: "How long have you been a financial planner?" (And get proof.) "How long have you lived in the community?" (Check it out.) Get references from two or three clients (but be sure they are clients and not uncles and neighbors). Ask about the financial trade organizations he belongs to and check their veracity and standing. Contact your state securities administrator before considering placing investments with anyone, even if your best friend vouches for this person. A financial advisor can well afford to misjudge the market—with your money!

The American Economy— a Contradiction in Terms

LUNGE HOUR

You see her Bloomingdaley
She shops and chatters gaily
Up and down the escalator
An economic indicator
She gives her all
But can't come close
To our "Consumer Spending Rose"*

There are two kinds of shoppers: those who avoid it and those who adore it. I fall in the cracks. I window shop. It fascinates me. The repeat performance of styles swamps my memory, sometimes with waves of nostalgia. I cannot, for example, pass a case of antique jewelry without looking for the lovely brooch Charlie had given me, which was swept up, along with every precious piece I owned, by a heartless burglar. I do choose gifts I give myself. But sometimes I "shop" in my own storehouse of treasures. When I wanted my new grandson to give his Mommy something special on her first Mother's Day, I selected a lovely silver box I had laid away for just such a purpose. The hastily wrapped and ribboned gift was unveiled to oohs and ahs, and when the little silver lid was raised, it revealed an honorary medal presented to me by the Daughters of the American Revolution. Life's embarrassing moments!

Selecting a present for a man has its difficulties, too. Either he already has everything for his hobby, sport, or habit and doesn't care for sartorial trappings; or he has no hobby, sport, or habit and buys his own wardrobe. Women are much easier to please, partly because fashions change, seasons change, waistlines change, and household appliances change. For older people, other factors enter into thoughtful gift-giving. They have completely equipped homes; newfangled items don't thrill them; they've started to divest themselves (by more circumspect methods than I!) of the overload of a lifetime accumulation of things.

But we still want to give pleasure, remember, celebrate, honor an occasion, event, or holiday. Perhaps the only factor to consider is the smile that the choice of gift can elicit. It's never "too late" to buy something silky-lacy for a lady. Never choose a gift for your spouse that you wanted—be it car, camera, or carafe. It won't be appreciated. Men should not buy clothing for women. They have no idea how long it takes her to choose the right thing—hours, days, months sometimes. No man has that much patience. He may not realize that "way out" is in; but he could go to any length with a pearl necklace. Don't give a man another tie, sweater, or windbreaker. Instead, get the latest in a corkscrew and include an extravagant bottle of vintage wine—to share. Don't be practical; it's so boring. And try not to be too inventive. No one needs a pocket pepper mill. But almost everyone can enjoy a bird feeder hung outside the kitchen window, which will serve as a stage for the performance of neighborhood birds, even in the city.

Catalogue shopping is a form of window shopping. A $40 billion business. It's more than a convenience. It affords an opportunity to comparison shop without running from store to store. The illustrations and descriptions give more

information than one gets from most salesclerks. It is a fine
way for families to confer on purchases and arrive at decisions together, avoiding the public arena for settling their
differences. Returning merchandise is not only possible, it
is less inconvenient than standing in line in a retail store and
being given the third degree by an officious clerk. Catalogues are a great help to people who don't have access to
diversified metropolitan shopping areas. But there are
problems—not necessarily with the merchandise or seller.

The first danger to guard against is impulse buying. I
venture to guess that half of the $40 billion is spent on
merchandise not needed. Some special-interest mailings
address preselected customers, those with a specific hobby,
for instance. When garden catalogues come, it's difficult for
me to temper my preseason enthusiasm. I fill out the order
form, but then let it rest for a few weeks. Eventually, I cross
out a few items. A hidden problem in buying by mail is the
credit card. One is so much less aware of paying for
purchases when no money seems to be going out. Some
households, where several members use the same charge-
card number, find themselves in a precarious financial position when bills come in.

If there is a stack of bills on your desk that defy understanding, send them to Ralph Nader. No, he won't pay
them. He will use them to further his cause on your behalf,
the baffled consumer. It is his intention to make Congress
aware of needless complexity and downright inefficiency in
these unavoidable pieces of mail. One shouldn't have to
spend hours figuring, checking, or guessing what the bot-
tom line is. Merchants, banks, charge accounts, investment
firms, doctors—in fact, most billing and account statements
are so complicated and confusing that one tends to give up
and just pay. Or worse, one lets bills pile up and then finds
seventeen percent carrying charges tacked on (com-
pounded on a daily basis) and usually applied to new
purchases as well as old balances.

One would like to believe that with computerized billing
no error or fraud is possible. However, mistakes are made

by computers. To argue with a machine is fruitless. Bills from hospitals, telephone companies, and automotive repair shops cause consumers the most problems. Overcharges, lack of itemization, charges for services not rendered, merchandise not bought or delivered. Do you know what is meant by a processing charge? Well, it means you are being charged for having the bill *sent* to you! There are ways to avoid all this: Pay cash. Or, become a tireless private bookkeeper to yourself and maintain infallible records, against which to check all bills and account statements. Never pay what you can't figure out. If the wording confuses you, demand an explanation. "Insist on plain English," says Nader. "If sellers say they are simply following standard practice and you're the first to complain, tell them you're used to being first and, as with Columbus, others will follow."

One side effect of television is impulse buying. I am concerned about that segment of the buying public whose favorite programs unfold in an atmosphere of such opulent splendor that all the world is made to feel just a smidgen above the poverty line. For compulsive spenders, this can become disastrous. According to a woman who makes it her business to help others cure this addiction, they do not realize the difference between needing and wanting. Sandi Gostin almost ruined her own life with uncontrolled spending. It even landed her in jail, after a conviction of embezzlement and parole violation. She could find no one to help her conquer her spending habit. So, she was forced to create her own mousetrap. She calls her support group "Spender Menders." A public service announcement brought so many calls that she almost lost her voice talking to people who needed help. Seventy percent of the population is financially overextended, now that buying on credit is available to virtually everyone.

We are a young country, with a booming economy. Things become old so quickly that we had to invent garage sales. There you can find the marvels of recent history— electric knives, plate warmers, pressure cookers—proof of the power of advertising. "You still have a Flintstones word processor?" eventually pressures us into acquiring an updated model of an item we didn't quite know what to do with in the first place.

To witness conspicuous consumption in its most highly developed form, stop in at a bath and kitchen remodeling showroom. On a Saturday. In an upscale trading area. The parking lot is crowded with late model cars, which bring husband and wife teams, in matching $250 denim. The opulent bathroom displays would drive Caesar to plunder. Closet components so luxurious, the latest line is called "Esmalda." Couples with remodeling fever feast their eyes on imported kitchen cabinetry, invisible cook tops, refrigerators that might mix cocktails, travertine countertops. The conversations are more ludicrous than on any sitcom.

The pristine kitchens are usually coveted by folks who eat out at least four nights a week and buy prepared conveniences from caterers and delis for the occasional "at home." It is unlikely that cooking for the sake of economy is part of the redesign scheme. These kitchens cost more than $700 a linear foot. Multiplied by the space in an affluent, suburban kitchen, figure $10,000 to $14,000—not counting state-of-the-art appliances, French tile floors, wood ceilings, built-in lighting, sinks, replacement windows, and skylights. Oh yes, we must have skylights. These will make the place so hot on a summer afternoon that air-conditioning becomes requisite. Colonial kitchens were in the cellar, perhaps for that reason.

Most people have perfectly adequate kitchens and bathrooms now, which have served them well for the ten, twenty, thirty years they have lived in their present homes. Why this drive for improvement? To enhance the real-estate value? To indulge in harmless hedonism? Out of boredom? To gratify the edifice complex!

It never ceases to amaze me how fashion innovators know we will buy musty-colored sports tops; cutoff sweatshirts, with seams sewn wrong-side out; fabrics that are perma-*wrinkled;* work boots; and fatigue pants. Faded jeans are

being worn with gold lamé blouses or garish sequined but-
terfly designs. Sweaters *must* be four sizes too large. And
(yes, I've seen it) pantyhose with paint splashes or carefully
spaced *holes*. These duds are for people who have never
known real deprivation. We are so thoroughly self-indul-
gent that only making *fun* of ourselves can squelch the guilt
of conspicuous consumption. Inflation is down to the single
digits and the gross national product climbs steadily. Just
the same, it might be wise to look back a little. I remember
being presented a plate of fresh fruits and nuts and a new
wool hat for Christmas—and being thrilled.

The post-War children of post-Depression parents are
probably the most indulged generation on record. They
perpetuate that life-style with their children. Suburban
homes with a bedroom per person and private bath, as well.
Electronic sound systems in every room. After-school lessons in sports, music, language (and remedial reading?).
Children shop on credit and are banished to summer camp.
We were at fault. We bought our children expensive educa-
tions and cars, with which they drove right off the edge of
reality. Now they must diet because we force-fed them every
conceivable edible and tangible delicacy. To no one's surprise, the new look in interiors is *minimalism* (bare floors,
naked windows, muslin covered couches, wire mesh chairs).
The kitchen has an antique 1930 gas stove, white cabinets,
thick coffee-shop dishes; and beds are left to look slept in.
Decked out like this must make it easier to face the real
world.

* Marion Glasserow Gladney

Sound and Fury

Is there a law against thinking your own thoughts? We watch presidential debates and then wait for the analysts to tell us what we should think. We roam the aisles of supermarkets, while the public address system intrudes on our thoughts with the day's specials or clobbers our ears with soupy songs. We shop for a new skirt, plotting what to wear with it, while dog food commercials bark over the store's radio.

True, you don't have to rent earphones on airplanes. You might prefer to read or think. But when it's time for the film presentation, your choice is narrowed considerably. A request is announced that all shades be lowered for the convenience of the film viewers. Readers must rely on the overhead lamp, making it difficult to maintain your train of thought while a silent flick is distracting your peripheral vision. Recently, in-flight movies have begun to be preceded by numerous commercials, amplified over the PA system. Where can one find a commercial-free zone?

The privacy of a taxicab ride is also being invaded by the commercial world. As captive audience, paying passengers are now forced to watch flashing advertisements ostensibly because there's nothing else to do. Taxi-grams, they call it.

The second best thing to do in a taxi is to enjoy the solitude. The best is to talk to the driver. The variety of moods, accents, attitudes, and opinions is limitless. When you get to your destination—a meeting with an opposing lawyer or potential employer—you are never at a loss for a gambit when you quote a cabbie. One Italian cabbie, who haunted the Broadway district, was familiar to most theater folks. He auditioned during the ride, usually with something from Verdi, which is certainly more amusing than electronic advertising.

I love American enterprise, American business acumen, and economic structure. But please allow me to come to *it*. I don't want it following me. My ears are not for hire. My eyes are not for rent. And I certainly don't enjoy paying for having mercantile messages crowd my milieu. I like good conversation, as long as I'm included.

We carry on an inordinate number of conversations, every day, that are forced on us. However well we organize our lives and manage our time, there's one small apparatus that manipulates us. The telephone. We can shut off the alarm clock, ignore the doorbell, cancel appointments. We can take the car and disappear for days. Stay at home and pretend to be gone. But when the phone rings, we feel obligated to answer it. Of course, it can be unplugged, covered with pillows, or attached to an automatic answering device. But its power over us will remain. It is an intrusion, even if it never rings, because then it's a sulking admonition that we should be calling people.

Most phone calls—incoming or outgoing—are too long, too repetitious, too boring. I hope we're a long way from televised phone calls. I don't relish having it known how I overcome the tedium of telephoning. A long cord lets me move around the room, look out the window, pick dead leaves off the houseplants, search for a book on the shelf. (Does anyone make a cord that reels itself up like on a vacuum cleaner? It would be safer.) A shoulder rest attached to the receiver frees me to stitch a hem, straighten up a drawer, polish silver or fingernails. I don't think it's proper to watch television or read a magazine; I might forget who's on the line, while acknowledging the conversation with "You don't say," "Oh my!" "Is that so?" I do a few simple yoga stretches and sometimes hold the receiver in the other hand, to the other ear. It's very good training to counteract one-sidedness.

What was the worst part of going to school? Being called on by the teacher. A sudden rush of blood to the brain when your name was called invariably erased all memory, like a computer when the power fails. In spite of that universal experience of terror and forgetfulness, we are still called on, every day, to come up with the answer at a moment's notice, unprepared. The phone rings. When you reach for it, you don't know whether it's the Red Cross looking for a donation, the bazaar chairman soliciting merchandise, a friend inviting you for dinner, CBS with a "live recorded" interview, the Gallup Poll, or sad news about a dear relative. It is impossible to be prepared with truth or white lies for thousands of situations.

I long for the return of the days of letter writing. No phones, no magnetic tape recording, no instant video playback. I wish people would not ask me if I saw last night's TV show or interview. It makes me feel uninformed, tuned out, almost reclusive to say I didn't. I crave thinking time. When I read a book, I can let it rest on my lap and reflect about it; maybe reach for another book to look something up. I can let my mind idle on a specific passage, race back, or ahead, or in circles. I can take a pad and pen and write what reading brought to mind. You can't do that when you watch TV, listen to the radio, talk on the phone, play tapes, and use headphones. Electronics are drowning out thought. It's all *instant* and about as nourishing as a $1.49 *butter* cake mix before you add a quarter pound of butter and three eggs. I prefer to enrich my life with a minimum of prepackaged goodies.

It is not possible to legislate against bad taste. The tendency is to wish for governmental interference when blatantly offensive material influences our youth. But, that is not how our country operates. Some musical records and tapes carry warnings that lyrics are morally hazardous. "Parents' Music Resource Center," a Washington-based group, seeks adoption of controls and regulations of rock lyrics. Founded by Mrs. Tipper Gore, wife of the senator from Tennessee, it is supported by the wives of a dozen powerful congressmen and government officials. It is their contention that some musicians and performers have become "Pied Pipers of evil." Can a rating system help in any way? I doubt it. Labeling of this kind only draws attention to the explicitly obscene and violent material parents would prefer not to have drummed into the ears and subconscious of their children. Can "parental guidance" ratings deter production or control purchasing? It's unlikely. We are a nation where free enterprise flourishes. Restraint of trade is antithetical to our way of doing business. Freedom of speech and artistic expression guarantee that we will have good, bad, and horrendous. Many of the lyrics in rock music are incredibly offensive, blatantly obscene, profane, violent, sexually explicit, crude, brutal, cruel. Some glorify the occult; others advocate drug and alcohol use. How damaging it is is difficult to judge. It must numb the habitual listeners' sensitivity and sensibility.

I'd like to suggest that people who write, sing, produce, and distribute such material be put in a position where they must explain and defend their product. On exhibition, so to speak. Every TV and radio talk-show host and interviewer should invite them to expound on the entertainment value of their creative output. It would be revealing to also interview all age groups of collectors of such recordings. Let's hear what they have to say, what kind of people they turn out to be.

Thomas Alva Edison started the whole thing when he yelled for Watson. Ever since then, all you hear is "What's on?" As recently as five years ago, no one could have convinced me that I'd live to see Americans walk around with antennae coming out of their heads and wires strung from their pockets to their ears. One grandfather thought his grandkids would like him a whole lot more if he had buttons on his ears and wires running down his pant legs.

The more music there is around, the less people sing or play an instrument. Free music—all day, all night—in public places, at home, in transit, at work. I never hear anyone hum a tune, much less sing a song. Do families still buy pianos, except when a ten-year-old is about to be offered up as a sacrifice to the keyboard? Do mature adults still make music for their own pleasure?

To create sound is not quite the same as listening to it. In the beginning of this century, we entertained ourselves with ingenious inventions like hand-cranked Victrolas or pianos that ran on pedal power. And we made music from scratch, with musical instruments and our God-given vocal cords. This is how John Philip Sousa saw it in 1906: "It must be admitted that, where families lack time or inclination to acquire musical technique and to hear public performances, the best of these machines supply a certain amount of satisfaction and pleasure." And he went on to express what, I fear, is now rattling his tombstone: "But, I foresee a marked deterioration in American music and musical taste . . . by virtue, or rather by vice, of the multiplication of the various music-reproducing machines." Thus, he was prophetically fearful of "all manner of revolving things," as he called machine-made music, available in 1906.

So, we don't have sing-alongs. We play games. Trivial Pursuit is it! Nothing else can even come close to turning a gathering into congenial togetherness. It's absolutely logical that "trivial" is the current focus for mental stimulation and amusement. We are not only avoiding the present and its realities, we have pulled the plug. Experts in the field of social research are finding that Americans of all ages are "turning their backs on national and foreign policy issues." We react to these events the way we do to a book that's difficult to understand—we don't try. Much of what we read and hear is simply incomprehensible. How can there be more hungry people in our own country than twenty years ago, when the economy is said to be making huge strides forward? How can we worry about Africa, when we can't understand why there are crumbled vagrants huddled in the doorways of our cities?

"Social gatherings," says Dr. Jonathan Fanton, the president of the New School for Social Research, "no longer seem legitimate places to exchange views on world affairs." We've become inured to crisis reporting, to which we are subjected day and night. "You give us twenty minutes, we'll give you the world." Every twenty minutes! Most people can't take on more issues than their own complicated lives already present. "We are seeing a backlash to the glut of information," says the editor of a newspaper in a town of two thousand people.* No one reacts; no one mentions; no one responds to even the most critical issues of the day. Not only do we feel our involvement would not make the least difference, we are also never entirely sure that we are given enough information and all of the truth to help us comprehend. The result is that "many people are going for easy politics and certain answers."† Sociologists and pollsters are seeing a national turnoff.

Since most of us are transported from one place to another in relative comfort, one wonders at the weather forecast mania. Or, as one wag put it, quite accurately, "weather post-dicting." One cable TV station boasts fifty-two friendly weathercasters who update the heavensent news every five minutes. "Live Weather Watch Is Now in Effect. Don't take a chance on the weather." If there is one thing I want to take a derring-do chance on—it is the weather. I can't imagine opening my eyes in the morning and not first peering at the sky to see what is going on out there. Or sniffing the air to decide how it suits me. Or looking at the thermometer to guestimate what might be on the way.

The uninterrupted, all-day weather channel promises to deliver instant weather warnings. Weather outlook, weather update, weather watch. How about a weather wrap-up? "Today's weather conditions appear to have conformed to expectations. The sun rose, as predicted, precisely at 6:02 A.M. The heavy cloud cover we witnessed this morning did

eventually release the prespoken precipitation . . ." and so
forth. Weatherpersons love to dramatize conditions, which
are totally beyond their control, in any case. They may yet
drive us underground in abject insecurity. (There already is
a city being built under a dome, in preparation for moon
living.) Current conditions are flashed on as *news*. Open the
window and take a current look! I really don't want to know
how things are in London—until I get there—or in Ken-
tucky, unless I'm concerned about the growth rate of blue-
grass. Boating and aviation weather advisors are more accurate at marinas and airports. I, for one, would never cancel
vacation plans because they tell me it rained there.

We are connected through airwaves. So many homes have
televisions and radios going all day. Even if no one is watching, children *hear everything* and absorb the impact of terror
and drama. It disturbs them far more than one realizes—but
only up to a point. Sooner or later they will become conditioned—as we all are—and will be immune to the natural
rhythm of life that was meant to bring people together.

---

* New York *Times*, March 1985, Columnist Charlotte Curtis (town of
Unalaska, Aleutian Islands)
† Dr. Willard Gaylin, psychiatrist and president of the Hastings Institute of
Society, Ethics and the Life Sciences

This Is My Country

Cement castles are what high-rise hotels try to be. Architects who design these parallelograms-within-parallelograms, *ad infinitum,* seem to get their inspiration while staring out their design studio windows through venetian blinds. Every time I arrive at such a pleasure palace, I scan the multibalconied facade, looking for signs of life behind uniformly drawn draperies. It looks like hundreds of mail slots to me. And now, they'll put me in there, and it'll be like the dead-letter office: No one will ever come to claim me. And yet, I travel.

The most accomplished actuarian could not calculate the number of hotels, castles, inns, motels, and rooming houses in which I have stayed during the years of theater and worldwide visiting since I was five years old. There is only one thing wrong with traveling as much as I do. I miss my house, my garden, my friends. But don't think that will ever stop me. There is too much out there for me to see and do. I am a glutton when it comes right down to it; I cannot get enough of the wonders of the world.

Alaska! What a feast for the eyes is that most northerly corner of our country. No moviemaker's special effects crew could ever imitate it. I took a walk once, all by myself, at New Winds when my shipmates went off by train to Anchorage. I was just walking alongside the railroad tracks and suddenly, there it was, an honest-to-goodness glacier: pure, clear, aquamarine in color, awesome in size, a frozen tidal wave. The glacier and me; nobody else around for miles. What did I do? I greeted it: "Hello, I'm Helen Hayes. Fancy seeing you here!" And then, I heard a bit of crackling. It may have answered me.

On an organized side trip from the ship *Saga Fjord,* we were taken by bus to a big glacier outside of Juneau. We passed a river that was clogged with red salmon, which had been spawning. They had traveled up that river and were exhausted from their trip. Up above, on the high ground, sat a flock of great American bald eagles, those somewhat lazy predators (perhaps not the best choice to symbolize our nation). They were perched there like pigeons in a San Francisco park, just waiting to get hungry enough to pick off a bit of fresh salmon for lunch—a veritable smorgasbord delicacy. Such are the laws of nature! They are beautiful birds soaring high above, riding the thermal air currents or diving down for a meal. It is part of the thrill of seeing the real Alaska—the most spectacular scenery of lush green and icy blue, of rivers and fields and wildlife. And, only two percent of it has ever been tampered with by man.

I wonder if I am far off the mark if I say that most Americans know the Mississippi only through the writings of Mark Twain. Except, of course, those of you who live there. And then, there are those of us enthusiasts who take to that most majestic of all rivers by steamboat. I'm absolutely hooked on it and have been a passenger on the *Delta Queen* many times.

There is a great saga about this stalwart little boat that ventured forth into the open sea, and she most definitely was not constructed for that! She was built for service on the Sacramento River, north of San Francisco. Then she was laid up for many years. In her second career, her marvelous captain, Fred Way, brought her down the Pacific Ocean from San Francisco to the Panama Canal, to get her to the Caribbean Sea, and then from there to the Gulf of Mexico to enter the Mississippi at New Orleans. There used to be hundreds of steam-driven side-wheelers and stern-wheelers on our great rivers and lakes. But, fortunately, we still have the *Mississippi Queen* and the *Delta Queen*.

One of the great sights on the Mississippi River is the run from St. Louis to St. Paul, on the upper river. That is as high as you can go by ship. After the first day out, you go through twenty-seven locks built by the U. S. Army Corps of Engineers—a miracle of engineering, in which Americans can take great pride. You pass barges loaded to the gunwales with cotton, coal, gravel, lashed together—three rows of four or five barges. They are pushed or pulled along the wide river by impertinent little tugboats with fanciful, feminine names. It is a part of river life that has not disappeared.

To really get to know Huck Finn country, view it at the lazy pace of a riverboat. But the pace is not always slow. The two *Queens* of the Mississippi have an annual race, for which I have served as one of the judges more than once. Much of the excitement and entertainment is provided through nature's special effects. You will never see more spectacular sunrises or more dramatic sunsets anywhere in the world. The river is a holdout in the American landscape. The surrounding country along the banks has not changed nearly as much as most places. It still has a bit of early Americana. Hear a calliope or banjo-playing by musicians whose talents have been handed down the family tree. Yes, they still call out "mark twain" when they gauge the water's depth with twine, and it is true that "once you wash your hands in the Mississippi, you'll always come back."

On a par with the splendor of the river is the Grand Canyon. Have you ever seen it? Not one photograph or essay can do it justice. It is one of the most stupendous natural places we have in the world. No matter how many times it has been illustrated or filmed, you somehow never realize how surprising it is. When you first see it, you feel that you, personally, have discovered it. The canyon takes you completely by surprise. You drive from Phoenix, or the eighty miles from Flagstaff, Arizona, across flat, uninteresting country and keep saying "Where is it? There's nothing here! It can't be much!" And then, suddenly, there it is, this gargantuan cleft in the land of astounding, incomprehensible proportions and colors. A thousand pictures cannot recreate the impact of actually standing there at the South Rim. Trying to absorb—with your eyes, ears, skin—the power of this place is almost more than you can bear. You have to turn your back on it to catch your breath. Turn around and the light has changed, clouds have moved, the thousand architectural, sculpted shapes have regrouped, been repainted. Shadows create new angles; wind and river orchestrate the drama. The curtain never descends. Second show at sunset. Midnight and sunrise are gala performances. The birds are part of the supporting cast. And so are the tourists. Yes, they add something vital: We see our own, infinitesimal proportions and speak in one voice but a dozen languages—spectacular!

I don't always travel alone. But it did take some time to get over my prejudice about group travel. In some ways, I now like it better. When I am with a good guide, I know I see the best and don't worry that I miss something important. I like sharing the wonders and oddities; that is my joy of traveling in parties. I am an unabashed tourist myself, and I don't hate tourists. "Oh these crowds," complained my friend at the Acropolis. I told her: Remember, this place was created for all of Greece—and the whole world—to come and enjoy. It was crowded in its heyday (with a lot of Greeks!). We are tourists, all of us. The native population hates it when we put on airs.

When I travel, I want to experience regional flavors. The kinds of restaurants that never get a write-up in some ways are the best. They exist on almost every street and highway and don't keep the same hours as the rest of the world. All-night diners. Early morning truck stops. What they dispense is comfort, coffee, and conversation. Waitresses in these places are professional mothers. They know most of their odd-hour clientele by name and don't need to give out menus. The people who frequent these places don't vary their nutritional needs from day to day. Not their concerns, either. The best bacon and eggs are guaranteed. The apple pie is local. Pork chops are juicy. Coffee cups get refilled with an accurate splash, unasked for. You don't have to request a glass of water. The service is hardly ever surly; if it is, the customer probably deserved it. Tipping is remarkably generous, considering the size of the checks. Credit cards are not welcome; receipts are rarely requested.

Eateries with names like "Mike and Myrtle's" are owner-operated, staffed by waitresses who have been there twenty-five years, with no thought of ever retiring. In indestructible nurses' shoes and pink or blue polyester pants and tops, they keep on their feet half the night or day, depending on the shift. Why? Probably because they need the human contact as much as electricians, rig drivers, secretaries, and factory hands need a square meal and the rough but real treatment they came for. Somehow, one feels more comfortable there than in any four-star, high-toned spot in town. You belong; it's like family. No one is obliged to impress anyone. The smiles, joshing, and genuine concern are in no way related to the size of the tip or the vintage of the car parked out front. Many years ago, I was given the recipe for scooped-out Idaho potatoes mixed with grated cheese, fresh parsley, and crumbled bacon and butter. It's still on my party menus.

I do quite a bit of armchair traveling between trips. I read books about places I have seen, and not seen, and I get travel fever. Revisiting favorite, old places can be disappointing. One returns to a familiar place after some years and can't recognize it. Everything has changed. Small buildings are replaced by skyscrapers. The farm is now a mall. The ranch has evolved into a fish farm. The park is an industrial park. Hills are leveled and rivers rerouted. Rural regions sprout corporate monoliths in an ocean of cars. Outlying districts are covered by the ooze of urban sprawl.

Macadam rolls out by the millions of miles, bringing us within easy reach—of what?

"Parks provide people with a sense of stability," says William Penn Mott, Jr., director of the National Park Service. His arrival in Washington made conservationists, like myself and my friends, hopeful. Mott is the man who expanded the California park system when he had the chance. A preservationist, he advocates national park *expansion:* a "Tall Grass Prairie" park for Oklahoma, a "Great Basin" park for Nevada. He proposes land acquisition to help protect the Florida Everglades. Big Sur in California is high on his priority list. The problem is he's just not getting any support from the Department of the Interior. The Federal budget seeks to rescind millions of dollars already appropriated by Congress for parkland. Other priorities. Well yes, we all understand that. But have you ever seen cement destroyed to make a park? Or trees planted where there had been smokestacks? Has a shore drive ever been displaced by a recreation area? Off-road vehicle parking along the Cape Cod seashore is *still* under advisement. Bill Mott has a difficult assignment. He can use all the help he can get, from you and me.

To tame nature is not only risky business, it is an idea that contradicts itself. Nature is, by definition, wild. We flatten mountains and thus create deserts. We harness rivers and deal death to the environment. Planes dive into the Grand Canyon and endanger the environment. The ocean does not tolerate containment, and the fire within the earth will never be capped. The Florida Everglades are an example of nature's answers to man's controls. "In the process of draining the Everglades, the developers reduced a natural work of art to a thing pedestrian and mundane," says Florida's governor Bob Graham, who is the force behind the Everglades reclamation program.

What is this place, the Everglades? Basically, it is a river, fifty miles wide and six inches deep, running 250 miles from central Florida to the state's southern tip, a great sheet of fresh water, supporting the most amazing wildlife. It is a fragile, three-million-acre ecological system that is nowhere duplicated. It supplies water to Miami and all of booming southeast Florida. Nearly lethal damage has been inflicted by a century of development and exploitation. Saving it means correcting past mistakes—turning back "progress" by one hundred years. In the 1950s and '60s, the Army Corps of Engineers dug a fifty-mile canal for the Kissimmee River, eventually devastating the natural balance within the wetlands. High on the restoration priority is the redirection of that river out of its arrow-straight channel, back into the old marshlands to recreate the fresh water supply. Alligators will swim again, and manatees, too. The mangrove trees will shelter eagles, ospreys, and vultures. And, at the water's edge, more pelicans, terns, gulls, cormorants, and sandpipers will congregate. There may be only twenty-two Florida panthers left. I hope they can hold on till the job is done.

The Personhood
of Women

The darling of the Golden West, Lotta Crabtree, was an old woman when I had the good fortune to meet her, when I was twenty. She was still lively as a chipmunk. I hoped to hear from this veteran stories of her past, vignettes about her performances during the Gold Rush—about skits, songs, and Dickens's plays with which she entertained the forty-niners, standing on a barrel or wooden platform. No such luck. There were no stories about her adventures with prospectors, nothing about the glamour or hardships. Sitting there in the Hotel Tremont in Boston (which she owned and where no other actors or actresses were allowed to live), she talked only about other women who were making an impact in the world. The first woman truck driver, aviator, jockey. She was fascinated with the advances made by other women in odd careers. It was not because she regretted any part of her own life. I think doers don't reminisce. They want to stay involved with what is going on today, not live on memories. Now, in my time of relaxation, I find myself much like Lotta, fascinated by women's lives and career expansion.

People who know me well all agree I don't know how to

say no. A look at my appointment calendar confirms it. One friend went so far as to have a lapel pin made for me, which says simply "No." It's supposed to prompt me to utter this single syllable in moments of predictable weakness. It doesn't always work. I never had a support group. Total involvement among ambitious young women is now so prevalent that it spawned a San Francisco-based support group called "Superwomen's Anonymous." Its progenitor is Carol Osborn, thirty-seven, whose credentials read like an introduction at a tenth-year college reunion. She's president of a public relations firm; novelist; brown belt in karate; magazine columnist; wife of a country-and-western rock musician; mother of a six-year-old and a one-year-old, both of whom qualify as state-of-the-art children. Her older superchild takes instruction in soccer, religion, karate, music, gymnastics, scouting, French, skiing, swimming, and acting. (Mother does the carpooling.) They taught him to read by labeling every item in the house: CHAIR, TABLE, RUG —a mega-sized alphabet soup. Women like that mother, who are everything to everybody, are dubbed "Type E." (For excessive?) I would call them "Type I" for invincible, infallible, irrepressible. *In*sane!

But then, one day, Osborn put all this behind her. She invented "downward mobility." Yuppies take note. Join "Superwomen's Anonymous" for twelve dollars a year and receive a newsletter "guaranteed not to teach you how to cope, juggle, or manage—plus a membership card and poster with the group's motto: Enough is Enough. Members are required to bow to the poster before saying yes to any new obligation, assignment, or commitment." It's probably too late for me.

The one who buys the groceries, supplies the menu, sees to the needs and obligations of the children, manages and maintains the home, nurses the ailing, and supervises the whole establishment is officially not considered "head of household." That appellation automatically applies to the adult male member, who provides, it is assumed, the greater share of resources as primary wage earner. One young

housewife, in her first encounter with a census taker, was
offered this descriptive identification next to her name:
household executive. You bet! That's pretty accurate for
women who juggle the complications of family, feeding,
electrical contrivances, transportation, and hygiene with a
memorized flow chart. Today's census forms require that a
"householder" be identified. It refers to the *one* person in
whose name the home is rented or bought, or any adult
member who is responsible for the household. There
should be two acceptable answers. Both adults in a family
are heads of household, each with his or her own sphere of
influence and responsibility. Women are no longer to be
thought of as dependents, or as members of the unpaid,
uncounted work force of domestics. What is happening to
women, both in the workplace and the home, is happening
fastest in the United States. There are now more than
100,000 women earning over $100,000 a year. But only ten
percent earn more than $20,000, even though more than
half of all adult females bring home paychecks. They still
earn only sixty-two cents to the dollar a man is paid for
comparable work.

To be a political democracy, it is encumbent upon us to
be an economic and social democracy. The concept "productivity" must take on an expanded meaning to include
home duties, part-time work, and volunteer activities, not
only full-time employment. Gone are the days when soap
operas asked: "Can a woman over thirty-five find romance?" Now the question is: "Can she find a job just like a
man, or, if she chooses, make householding a respected
occupation?" We are embarked on a wonderful adventure
in human development. The personhood of women.

In Jewish orthodoxy, men say a morning prayer that
blesses God for not having created them women. It's an
ancient prayer, which no doubt had its reasons. Today, one
can hardly blame them for such gratitude. Modern women
in midlife are caught in a revolving door: as wife, mother,
daughter, and job holder. They are responsible for their
households, their children, and their husbands' comfort. In

addition, they take on the responsibility for the aging parents in the family. Just when they are looking ahead to a freer time in their lives—when they may start or resume a career—a new, unexpected choice is thrust on them: career or caretaking. The latter is what sociologists call a gender-assigned task. The menfolk in the family may get involved with the financial aspect of caring for their parents. But daughters tend to do the laborious, time-demanding tasks.

Most adults would rather maintain their parents in their own homes than institutionalize them. In the last thirty years, the sixty-five-year-old population has doubled, and it will double again in the beginning of the next century. How many will be afflicted with protracted, chronic ailments? Daughters are more likely than sons to take grandparents into their own homes. And if the elderly manage to maintain independent dwellings, it's the daughter in the family who does the shopping, cleaning, transportation, and hiring and firing of household aides. As long as it is the accepted attitude that men hold the more important, less flexible jobs, the prevailing arrangements will never change. What man dares tell his boss he'll come in late because he has to take his mother to the doctor? And how are women perceived in the job market because they must frequently say things like that? It affects their careers, their salary levels, and advancement opportunities. We stop working to be mothers. We stop working to be daughters. A revamping of intergenerational attitudes is called for.

It takes a certain audacity and courage to become successful. For a woman, a married woman or one who would like to be married, it takes more than that. More than two-thirds of women twenty-five to fifty-four years old are in the labor force. Forty percent of law students are women. (It was four percent not long ago.) Women in all professional fields represent fifty-two percent. A significant number of those who are wives are more successful than their husbands. In show business, this has always been quite common. Yet who knows whether the marital turnover in that society isn't, in part, due to irreconcilable career differences. Historically, we are products of the work ethic that decrees that man brings home the bear, bacon, or bank book.

Family counselors, group therapists, and theologians have a new dilemma to deal with: when the wife's career advances outstrip those of her husband. Income and status, title and position are the recognizable signposts in business and the professions. A husband is often uncomfortable, even threatened, by a wife's career achievements. He knows it is unreasonable to feel this way, so guilt oversalts the mix of confused emotions. The woman may not permit herself to fully relish the pleasure to be derived from her success. She, too, feels a sense of guilt. It will take time and effort to break through polarized sex roles.

Women may have left home, but I think there's a menace afoot to put us back in it: computer terminals. Once they have convinced every man this new electronic genie must become a household member, they will be well on the way to putting us in our place—again. We will shop by computer, monitor the children, attend classes, hold down our *other* job, cook, launder, clean, and visit friends—all via TV terminal. Relaxation, entertainment, exercise, and of course, all information and education will come our way through the "monitor." "One that admonishes, cautions, reminds," explains the dictionary. How appropriate!

There was a time when the housebound woman had her mind manipulated by the printed page—every word geared to—that's right!—keeping her in her place. The nineteenth century abounded in magazines and periodicals just for these women. They were filled with stories, advice, and lessons entirely based on the notion that women had nothing on their minds but their domestic chores, their appearance, and their families. An ad for McCall's dated 1933 headlines this editorial: "Every Woman Leads a Triple Life. It's astonishing how many different people are rolled into one to make the average wife!" A ray of hope? The writer saw us in an expansive light? Not quite. In bold type, the triple threat is explained: "First, recreation and romance.

Second, her family life, her children. Third, her person, her clothes, her skin, her figure."

Women have problems that have no name. Still. We are only halfway there. In the TV miniseries *A Woman of Substance,* Emma Hart builds a one-woman business empire at a time in history—in Victorian England—when women could not own much more than the clothes on their backs. Not until 1975 did our Congress pass the Equal Credit Opportunity Act. What took so long? Attitudes, such as that women cannot be trusted with money, they have no head for figures, they don't pay their debts, and of course, that they are—and should remain—economically dependent on men. Well, not Emma Hart. Nor most women I have known well enough to like.

The congressional act "makes it illegal for creditors to discriminate against anyone because of sex or marital status. Specifically, women can obtain credit in their own names; they cannot lose their credit rating when they marry, nor when widowed or divorced; alimony and child support are to be considered as income; creditors must consider a wife's income when evaluating a couple's credit worthiness." If a woman is denied credit, the law requires that reason for refusal be made clear to her. Is one an ideal credit risk if one always pays on time and takes pride in never owing or buying on credit? Yes and no. Without a credit history, women have a devilish time getting credit. Apply for a charge account, credit card, car loan, personal loan, or mortgage, and suddenly one's credit experience, or lack of it, will become a major factor. Everyone's credit file is available nationally to those who extend credit. It is also available to consumers under the Fair Credit Reporting Act. If credit is denied, perhaps incorrect information is dogging you. It can be rectified and deleted if you know about it. To review your own file, look in the Yellow Pages for the "Credit Reporting Agency" that maintains files in your area. Every woman should establish a credit history in her own name and protect it with good business sense.

We no longer define status within the family by age, sex,

or purse power. We have made ourselves equal, with no one
at the top, and none relegated to other levels, either. Nor-
man Rockwell put yesterday on canvas. There is not always
a mother in the kitchen now. No clearly defined head of
household, ready to slice the bacon *he* brought home. No
elders to share, cherish, and respect. Children are no longer
considered chattel. Women are not unpaid servants. Men
are not all-powerful, and the rich are not served by peons.

Being set adrift, each in our own little skiff, is an unset-
tling environment in an era where four-generation families
are not at all unusual. At the far end of the spectrum is the
employed grandmother, who has a parent of her own still
living and a husband who wants to retire. The middle family
has two career people. That husband resents the housework. The wife's success undermines his self-image. The
children, depending on their ages, are in day care or after-
school enrichment programs. Or, they are latchkey kids,
expected to do the marketing and start the evening meal.
Then, perhaps with some luck, this family assembles for
what today is called "quality time." But I wonder. Can din-
nertime ever again be what Rockwell painted and many of
us romanticize as the good old days? "The family has been
shaken by mobility, two-career marriages, single parent
homes, grandparents in segregated housing, and divorce.
The losses at home seem to outweigh the gains in the world
at large."*

"Most people have a way of mistaking their prejudices for
the laws of nature," writes Ashley Montagu.† Women, he
feels, are just now beginning to emerge from their long and
unjustified period of subjugation. Our biological unique-
ness pays us with bouncing checks. Five years before our
country's independence, the 1771 edition of the *Encyclopae-
dia Britannica* covered the subject, women, in six words:
"The female of man, see Homo." Have we come a long
way? The 1945 Charter of the United Nations included only
thirty-six countries in the whole world that gave women
equal political rights. In its present form, our Constitution
guarantees women only the right to vote! Since 1948, we've

been trying to amend it, asking for nothing more than "equality of rights under the law (which) shall not be denied or abridged by the United States or by any other state on account of sex." But, at this moment, medieval law still governs women. We have the constitutional rights we had in 1789—not more. We are so highly prized, says Montagu—in fact, superior—that males must use it against us in order to feel less inferior. School books, as recently as just a decade ago, depicted girls as docile, timid, sedentary, helpless; and boys as heroic, sportive, productive, active, strong. And, the Constitution still reads: "All men are created equal." And that, ladies and gentlemen, excludes women. Too many men, and women, think the feminine revolution has been won. They now say: "I'm not a feminist. But . . ." We are in the "Second Stage," writes Betty Friedan; *the feminine issue is the family.* Tennyson understood: "Woman's cause is man's. They rise and fall together."

* *By Youth Possessed*, Victoria Secunda, Bobbs-Merrill Co., New York, 1984
† *The Natural Superiority of Women*, Ashley Montagu, Collier Books, New York, 1974

The Pendulum Swings

The pendulum swings. No sooner were the young content to live together in relative harmony (without benefit of clergy) than way-out weddings became all the rage. In the garage. On motorcycles. On a hill overlooking a prairie, dressed in natural flax or cotton, if not altogether *au naturel*. And, since nuptial knots cannot legally be tied in the air, one couple took their vows on the Tarmac beneath the wings of a small plane before going aloft to start their marriage made in heaven. Now the traditional wedding is back, glitzier than ever. The groom *owns* his tuxedo. His bride orders a beaded white gown with Belgian lace and yards of train. Wedding business at the Ritz Carlton Hotel in Boston has tripled in two years. Elegance, chandeliers, and lots of imported champagne. Gone are the days of health food and carrot cakes; we are back to a six-tier confection topped with the loving couple in effigy. The bride tosses her bouquet to the hopeful. The groom tosses the bride's garter to the stag line. The man who catches it fits it to the thigh of the young woman who caught the bouquet. The higher up it goes, the better are her chances.

Today's mother of the bride has less autonomy, especially

with a more mature bridal pair. Receiving lines are abandoned for reasons of complexity. The young couple may have acquired too many sets of parents, grandparents, siblings—dividends of divorces and remarriages of their elders or their own. Grooms no longer are led to the slaughter without a word. They have as much to say about the proceedings as the bride (and, formerly, her mother). As for elegant food and artistic flowers, less is more by current standards. When it comes to the final accounting, less is definitely more costly. In vogue again are bridal showers, bachelor parties, rehearsal dinners, bridesmaids, ushers, flower girls, and ring bearers. But table arrangements are less formal; round tables and no dais are considered friendlier. Decor and attire are either incredibly ornate or beguilingly simple. Goal-oriented Yuppies love the fantasy of a traditional marriage ceremony.

When a new trend is proclaimed, it is safe to assume the word "new" is out of place. Properly applied, it defines "what has just been found, discovered, or learned." Newness implies that something is fresh and has never before been done or used. We are told that dancing cheek-to-cheek is new. Well, not if you have been around for a while. Big shoulders and wide lapels are new. That means the suit I bought in Rio in 1947 is, again, perfect. Once it was the "poor boy" look in *haute couture*. Now it is the "starving artist," in rumpled, oversized shirt and leftover children's leggings. Fashion writers report that women go madcap over hats. Isn't that what we have always gone out to buy when we were good and mad? There are cycles even in medicine. A "new" approach to pain control is the mind-body connection. To yogis and Indian medicine men, that's old hat. Here is front page news: "Step-by-step learning raises the test scores of schoolchildren." That is not exactly a revolution, nor a revelation. Mastering a subject has always required a systematic application of drills and repetition.

New is a circle word. Everything eventually returns. Chart the stock market and it looks like a cardiograph. In personal life, nothing is really new either. The children leave and we are, again, just a pair—as we once were. If we are suddenly single again—well, we've been there, too. If your money supply begins to shrink, that is hardly a novelty; you've managed before. It is never a whole new ball game.

The return of Coca-Cola, the original, prompted a game: "What would you like to see come back?" Try it out on your friends. It is a lot of fun.

Wouldn't you like to see AT&T restored to its former, smooth-working convenience?

I certainly would like to see good, enduring dress and suit fabrics return to fashion. And pride in workmanship.

Self-entertainment is due for a rebirth. I wish people would, again, tune in to each other for news, for laughs, for drama, for games, for music—even for psychoanalysis, confession, and sympathy.

How nice it would be if all roads and buildings along beaches and river fronts around the world would melt, giving the natural splendor of these sites back to us.

I would like to see fire engines and police cars with bells again, in place of sirens.

To hear again the rhythmic rasping of a garden rake, instead of a leaf blower's screeching whine.

Hand-pushed lawn mowers to replace monster machines that break the sound barrier (and dig divots in my lawn). Hand-operated clippers and edgers that have a lazy summer cadence.

I'd like a year's subscription to *Theater Arts* for the 1943 price of $3.50 (half the cost of a single copy of some glossy publications today).

A suite at the Beverly Hilton, for $8.00 a night, the price when I played in *Harriet.*

Popular music used to have lyrics that rhymed; not only the words fit together, the sentiments echoed in our hearts.

I'd like a return to radio and television programs that are at least as fascinating as the commercials.

And, if only the moon could regain its former, *undiscovered* mystique!

Safe parks with neat park benches, so that gossip can again be transmitted from mouth to ear, not via satellite.

And here is one more: All the people who say "It's a piece o' cake" should actually know how to bake and enjoy doing it.

An Open Book

When education of the masses first became the universal aim, it was feared that too much knowledge was a dangerous tool. The English historian George Trevelyan said it would produce a vast population able to read but unable to distinguish what is worth reading. (What would he have said about televiewing, I wonder?).

Barbara Bush, wife of the Vice President, is trying to bring her national campaign against illiteracy to the attention of that segment of the public that still knows how to read: the Press. She appeals to journalists to "spread the word about the epidemic problem." Mrs. Bush shocks us into understanding the proportions by citing staggering statistics. Regarding literacy among civilized nations, America has dropped from eighteenth to forty-ninth place in thirty years. Newfangled electronic educational equipment seems not to stem the downward slide of literacy. An estimated 74 million Americans are either illiterate, functionally illiterate, totally unable to read or write, or reading at fifth-grade level. Fifty percent of the prison population is functionally illiterate. We keep them in jail at an annual cost of over $6 billion. We cut aid to education and don't seem to recognize the connection. Only about fifteen percent of juvenile delinquents who end up in court can read. What a waste of human spirit! As many as forty-seven percent of black youths are said to be illiterate. Danger lies in the prospect that it renders us powerless against tyranny. The English scholar Lord Brougham said: "Education makes a people easy to lead, but difficult to drive; easy to govern, but impossible to enslave."

A major national survey finds a twelve-percent drop in the reading habits of those under twenty-one. There is serious concern by educators (and publishers, no doubt) about the decline in book reading among school children. "It's especially alarming when you compare what's happening here to Japan, Cuba, or China, where most young people have developed the book reading habit."* If television, radio, Walkman, and Atari predominate in the home, there simply is no time for books. There is that essential difference when a five-year-old watches a classic movie like *The Wizard of Oz* or has it read to him. When he watches the celluloid version, his brain doesn't need to shift into drive, namely, imagination. Words no longer need to do the job for which they were intended. In the hands of a gifted writer, words can do more, much more, than the work of the most talented cinematographer.

Perhaps we should make a concerted effort to resurrect story time—at home and on television. Just reading! No animation, no dramatization, no sound effects. I might consider accepting the job of National Grandmother.

As a mother, I found endless rewards in stimulating my children's reading habits. I remember reading *Tanglewood Tales* to a very young Jamie. These Greek myths and legends, written by Hawthorne for children, fascinated him. Both front teeth were out at the time, and he lisped his correction to me when we talked of Hercules at lunch one day; his curly blond head hardly reached above the table. "That wathn't Herculeth; that wath Thetheuth." Jim turned out to be a very selective and avid reader. I take just a bit of credit for fostering it by nudging him into the mystery that

books hold. Mary, too, though she was a harder nut to crack.
She was satisfied to read her way through Nancy Drew—
only about fifty of those. But I got to her by introducing her
to Charlotte Brontë's Mr. Rochester. In the middle of *Jane
Eyre*, having built her curiosity, I feigned exhaustion, forcing her to finish the book on her own.

"The only degree you need is a degree of caring" is the
slogan with which the Advertising Council encourages us to
become involved in the fight against illiteracy. Members of
the Council, who are in business, advertising, and commu-
nications industries, contribute their skills and resources to
promote voluntary citizen action. The 27 million functionally illiterate adults are a national problem. What they don't
know hurts us all. They cannot read want ads, job applica-
tions, or street signs; the burden of their unproductive lives
falls on everyone. This is not a subculture, but friends,
neighbors, colleagues, and relatives—the "Drop-Outs of
the American Dream."

Nonreading adults develop most convincing methods for
hiding their lack of reading ability. Aware that they are
unlikely to respond to ads that offer tutoring, the campaign
provides a toll-free telephone number. The Contact Library
Center functions as a clearinghouse, referring teaching volunteers and new students to programs in their communities. "There is an epidemic with millions of victims. And no
visible symptoms." One third of the population: Voters.
Workers. Parents. Fifty to seventy percent of the unemployed are nonreaders. Illiteracy robs its victims of one of
life's most vital strengths, self-respect, and the pleasures
that come from reading, learning, or teaching their own
children. For a solution, look no further than within yourself. You can tutor, right in your community.

Literacy Volunteers of America has a membership of
more than 12,000 college students, lawyers, housewives,
teachers, retirees. Each tutor devotes a minimum of two
hours once a week to one student for a year. Some pupils
learn quickly; others have a lifelong reading block to overcome and it may take years before it is possible for a father

to read a storybook to his child or a mother to write a note to school. But what a triumph, for student and teacher, when it finally happens! Many had not been able to read menus, road maps, medicine labels, letters, bills, recipes, or even make a shopping list. For the nonreader, who often is the victim of neglected education and other great frustrations, the tutoring sessions in themselves are of great psychological value. It may well be the first time that anyone has paid that much attention to his needs and problems. For those of us who read without even being aware of it, it is difficult to imagine the blank screen that nonreaders have before their eyes. An illiterate mechanic may be a whiz at following diagrams because of his technical ability, but detailed instructions must be read to him. Literacy Volunteer tutors learn teaching methods in six mandatory three-hour training sessions and continue to improve their skills to "customize" teaching methods that will be most helpful to each student.

Herbert Spencer said that "reading is seeing by proxy." To me, it is living vicariously, conversing in solitude, escape, adventure without danger. Philadelphia classifies nearly forty percent of its adult population as "functionally illiterate." So slow in their reading skills, they are unable to deal with the printed word above the fourth-grade level. The mayor of Philadelphia is attacking the problem through the Commission on Literacy. Schools, colleges, churches, newspapers, television stations, and businesses all band together to support, organize, and publicize the adult reading program to combat illiteracy. So many can't read bus signs and street names that the 150 learning centers must be near their homes. "But, if all the people who need help came forward, there still wouldn't be enough places to put them."†

The author of *Why Johnny Can't Read* has followed his 1955 book with an update: *Why Johnny Still Can't Read.* ‡ Rudolph Flesch blames the "look-and-say" method for illiteracy in America. Fifty-five years ago, we abandoned the phonic method of sounding out letters. "With phonics-first, you

teach a child to read the word 'fish' by telling him the sound
of 'f,' about the short 'i,' and the 'shhh' of 's-h.' Then, you
tell him to blend the sounds from left to right to read the
word 'fish,' " To teach the same word by the "look-and-say"
system, you give the child a picture with the word printed
beneath. Visual ability and a good recall memory are cru-
cial, as is repetition, drill and, above all, guesswork. Change
the last letter in "fish" to "t" for "fist," and the little scholar
had better remember a different image. Thousands of pictures for thousands of words. But only twenty-six letters in
the alphabet! There is an alphabet code that applies to all
English words (with just a few exceptions). "It consists of
200 letters and letter groups, each standing for one or more
of the 44 sounds in English." Isn't that more reliable and
easier to learn than struggling with endlessly repetitious,
boring workbooks?

"The number of adult problem readers is increasing by
2.3 million each year." Flesch says, "Ever since 1500 B.C.,
wherever an alphabetic system of writing was used, people
have learned to read by simply memorizing the sound of
each letter. Except in twentieth-century America. We have
thrown 3,500 years of civilization out the window." Just
about every child should be able to read by the middle of
first grade and *enjoy* this glorious accomplishment for the
rest of his or her life.

*Leo Albert, Chairman of Book Industry Study Group, Vice President,
Prentice-Hall, Inc., New York *Times*, April 12, 1984
†Commission on Literacy, Mayor's Office, Philadelphia
‡*Why Johnny Still Can't Read*, Rudolph Flesch, Harper & Row, New York,
1981

Artificial Intelligence

There *was* education before the printing press. But for five hundred years now, the *printed word* has been the primary means to disseminate information. Technology has changed all that. The teacher is a screen and students are in charge; they push the buttons. The average American child spends at least twenty-eight voluntary hours each week with an electronic learning tool and perhaps twenty-five hours, mostly involuntarily, with the printed word. How will they be able to form mental images when everything that enters their minds has arrived there as a picture? When an actor or director is given a play or script to read, he forms the scenes in his head: motions, voice levels, lighting, costumes, scenery, colors, sound, and so on. An author has spent a lifetime perfecting the gift of stimulating mental images in his readers. Future generations will have only eyeball contact with their world. I am happy that right now, while you relax with a book, you are focused on that screen in the back of your skull where you can see what you choose to see.

Have you acquired a personal computer? Although it looks like a typewriter and acts like a TV, it sounds so complex that I can't imagine ever learning even the basics.

Ten-year-olds, on the other hand, can master the intricacies in jig time. I remember practicing the alphabet with chalk on a blackboard of genuine slate. Even in the '30s, some children still did their school work on a personal slate, framed in wood, which they carried back and forth, from home to school. The tears we shed if a scuffle in the school-yard broke the slate in our schoolbags! No homework to hand in. The old excuses—"The dog chewed it up . . ." "It rained on it . . ." "My little sister . . ." Only one excuse left for today's errant scholars: "Power failure."

There is talk of accelerating school, starting with four-year-olds and high school graduation at sixteen. Will learning still include the humanities? Will there be time? Microtechnology—everything you ever wanted to know on the head of a pin or through the eye of a needle. Who will sew on buttons while everyone is busily learning how to push them? An electronics ad proclaims, "The vendors of . . . hardware, software, micros, terminals, services, and supplies are faced with a monumental challenge: the sale and integration, this year, of $85 billion of information systems into every nook and cranny of corporate America."

I try not to complain about occasional lapses in memory. With a little effort, the word, name, or place will reappear, if not instantly, then later. And that's all right, too. It's a lot better than storing it all in a computer and worrying about an occasional lapse in electric power, which will wipe out the artificial intelligence. Imagine having all your personal and financial records stored in a computer that goes dead. Even the mattress would be a safer place. Computers are portable; even aboard an airplane, one can continue to work. One can organize recipes and Christmas lists. But why? What happened to pencil and paper? Can most people really think faster than they can write, or absorb information quicker than they can read? I can't.

Some broadcasts intersperse a few bars of music between news items; it gives listeners the rare chance to think about what was said and store it in the portable "software" located directly between the ears. Experts met on Cambridge campuses to examine the decline in thinking power, a conference attended by academicians and psychologists. The subject: *critical thinking.* Time must be made available to teach it *and* to practice it. One educator said: "I don't mind if the teaching of thinking becomes a fad, as long as it becomes part of the national consciousness." Artificial intelligence has its place in commerce and industry. For native intelligence to develop in the young, and function in adults, we may have to keep computers out of living rooms and classrooms.

How does one decide on a home computer? Do not ask the man who owns one. He and his family will swear by it, no matter what problems, technical and familial, they may have encountered. Expenditure mandates that they just love it and don't know how they ever lived without it. That may not be quite the truth, but why should they suffer alone! And then, there is the small matter of a fair-size investment. Home computers, usually referred to as microcomputers, range in price from less than $100 to several thousand, depending on how much they can do. A computer alone, however, is not very useful; it requires hardware—screen, storage devices, printer, etc.—and software that tells the computer what you want it to do. So, you are looking at several thousand dollars. For that, you should get convenience and ironclad assurance that repairs are available, that adequate software is provided by the manufacturer. Don't buy a thousand dollars worth of frustration. Computers are just machines and do only what they are told.

Brokers say soon there will be no stock certificates issued, just computer records of each transaction. Bankers predict that we are on the threshold of no bills piling up on our desks. Bank statements will record automated deductions for debts paid. The doctor will be able to punch the name or code into a keypad to read off each patient's medical history and that of his whole clan, as well. It is now possible for the state to have access to driver's license records to find out age, legal address, road violations, real estate holdings, and I don't know what else. In many incorporated villages, the

police have keys to the homes of subscribers to computerized security systems, which ostensibly help protect "for-
tress America."

The current heroes in this Buck Rogers turn of events are
a dozen seventeen-year-old boys in Milwaukee. The Bee-
thovens of our time are playing a different set of keys *and*
they are reading the score to the House of Representatives.
Neal Patrick and his friends, who "fool around" with computers (in a very sophisticated way, to be sure), managed to
break codes that allowed them to enter the computers of
Los Alamos Scientific Laboratory, Memorial Sloan-Ketter-
ing Cancer Center, and other spots around the country.
Native intelligence and intellectual curiosity prompted
them and made it possible for these young geniuses to
expose our society to its vulnerability. Young Mr. Patrick is
teaching us a valuable lesson when he says "the fact that we
were able to access shows the potential for damage. . . .
With sinister intent, the damage could run into the millions
of dollars. And that's just the dollar value," he adds, wisely.

Our government suggests that schools add an ethics sec-
tion to their computer courses. The U. S. Chamber of Commerce estimates white-collar computer crime has already
reached the $40 billion mark. If it *is* possible to teach com-
puter morality in the classroom, I guess it's time to give to
the college of your choice.

Owners of personal computers who actually master their
intricacies and possibilities run a serious risk of addiction.
Not everyone's PC lives up to the advertised promise, but a
few eventually do attain the status of household god. Ac-
cessing. What a remarkable idea it is that one can, from the
contoured comfort of one's chair, get information, day or
night, from almost anywhere. There are spouses who consider the PC a threat to marriage—a mistress, a lover—since
nighttime is best and least expensive for receiving or sending information over the phone lines. Some computer con-
verts acquire the pale complexion and red-rimmed, glassy
stares of casino denizens. I saw a gambler in Las Vegas who
carried a worn, patched pillow to ease the hours of sitting in

front of one-armed bandits, and whose right hand was padded and bandaged to cushion the impact of the lever. What auxiliary aids of this kind will soon come on the market for PC pack rats?

By the turn of the century, one third of the work force in industrialized countries will be "teleworking." This is a new term for a state-of-the-art cottage industry. No papers to file, no mail; not much telephoning, record keeping; no rushing off to work and business meetings. Telecommunications will link workers and employers, suppliers and clients, consumers and manufacturers. Millions of workers will be displaced by robots. Management will rely on electronic work stations. Your next new job may be in the room next to your kitchen. It is safe to predict that some of our most pressing social problems (childcare, eldercare) could be relieved by teleworking from home—for parents who want or must stay home, retirees who can be active and income-producing, for the aged who need caregivers. It will make the three- and four-generation household not only a likelihood, but a successful alternative to age segregation.

We've come a long way since smoke signals and carrier pigeons. What consequences will the computer age have on human contact, I wonder. With terminals in every home, we will no longer engage in any of those mundane activities about which we now grouse daily. Just drive by the supermarket and pick up the already bagged order, placed and paid for by the computer. You won't be chatting with your old neighbor in the grocery aisle, both of you trying to make life sound better than it is. Will we have to go to the office? Probably not. Every thought, order, wish, instruction, design can be automatically reproduced by facsimile machines, received in thirty-five seconds at the other end—supplier's warehouse, client's conference room, factory. No voice communication necessary, just digital electronic transmission. No long lunch, under the guise of closing the deal; no flirtation at the water cooler. Will schooling also be by computer, so that no one needs to dash for the bus; fidget in class; learn to deal with success, failure, reprimand,

and with friend and foe in the school yard? The image that comes to mind is an old daguerreotype, the whole loving family grouped around the hearth, in which, of course, flickers the read-out screen. One advantageous side effect would be utterly deserted highways at commuter time, empty trains and subways. But empty lives, too, I predict. If there is one necessity in life, beyond food and shelter, it is human contact—interchange of ideas (one-on-one), sound of voices (live), expressions on faces (not screens), touch and tone (human, not keypad).

Just as the telephone obliterates all visible elements of having communicated, so do we now lack ticket stubs, memorabilia of having attended a performance at a theater or concert. Tickets are usually charged to our account by computer and all we get is a flimsy chit—not a colorful souvenir. There are no mementos to paste in an album, which clearly show how we have progressed over the years from peanut gallery to loges. Katharine Cornell had an old multipane window made into a coffee table, where she arranged theater tickets and other souvenirs in shapes—spurs to so many wonderful memories.

For Mother's Day, a full-page ad offered a $4,000 robot as a suitable gift idea, obviously for the woman who needs nothing, from the man who has nothing to give.

We Built the
Twentieth Century

Do computers intimidate you? Does not grasping the difference between floppy and laser discs make you feel inadequate? Modern technology can give us an inferiority complex. Especially if we can't quite comprehend the need for automation of things we used to do without machines. Like laughing, before laugh tracks. Or running, before it was aerobics on a treadmill.

There never has been a time that spawned so much history and science. Those of us who have been around the better part of this century, we built the twentieth century. Social scientists call it the most dynamic in the history of humankind. We went from wagon wheel, to automobile, to rocket. We traveled from dirt road, to macadam, to the moon—and back. We spent decades and billions destroying what we built and building it again, sometimes better. We killed more people and created more new ones than ever before. We built taller, dug deeper, flew higher, and dove deeper. We sank more ships and raised some ancient ones from miles below the sea's surface. We permanently disposed of dread diseases and incubated new ones. We healed more bodies and harmed more minds. We've done more

good and ill with phenomenal technology. We split the
atom, nations, cities, and the family. We try to repair the
damage in what was once the remotest corners of the world.
Women moved from being owned to being owners, from
the disenfranchised to leadership, from slavery to management.

It is time now, with only a dozen or so years to go, that all
Americans realize that the elders created this astounding
era. We are the twentieth-century maturians. It was our
imagination, our thrift, our determination, our work ethics,
sacrifice, trial and error that made the United States the
preeminent nation of this century.

What is the basis of civilization? The very word gives the
answer: civility. We cannot live in groups and interact safely
and successfully unless we treat each other civilly. Caveman
discovered this quite readily. If he grabbed for the
shankbone being gnawed by his neighbor, he was sure to be
given a headache with it. How far have we come since then?
We call ourselves a civilization. Yes, if we mean by that the
music of the masters. The brushwork of geniuses. The sermons of the saintly. The word power of the gifted. The
philosophies of idealists. The inspiration of healers. And
even the discoveries of scientists—*unless and until* science
creates instruments of destruction . . . Medicine tampers
with creation . . . Words become propaganda . . . Philosophies defy logic . . . Preachments cause divisiveness
. . . Art incites . . . Music destroys the spirit.

We care a great deal about how we look. Most commercial
messages encourage us to improve our image. Not much is
said about how we sound or behave. We go through life so
beautifully dressed, coiffed, jeweled, perfumed—from our
perfectly appointed homes via sumptuous cars, to industri-
ally ideal work places. What is sorely missing, as we interact
with each other, is civility. Plain good manners. Caring
about the comfort of others. Knowing that some words do
make a difference. Surliness is the illness of our society,
especially in crowded, pressured urban centers. Ill-man-
nered behavior begets ill humor, ill temper, ill-treatment.

We don't seem to know any limits, when high-ranking government officials are quoted in the media with language not many would have used privately a few years ago. Justifiable anger does not justify uncontrolled language. Civilization will cease without civility. What do we hold sacred? People? Rivers? Forests? Air? Land? Oceans? Not much, if you look around.

Now and then, I spend a weekend in Texas at the LBJ ranch with Lady Bird Johnson. One of her prime concerns is the preservation of the wildflowers of our land. I think about her struggle when I see the devastation caused by municipal power mowers along parkways everywhere. All they accomplish is to create traffic jams, raise dust, expose the grass roots to the scorching sun, and clear away fragrant greenery so we can look upon the debris as we barrel along. Lady Bird and I reminisced about our childhoods and what flowers had meant to us then: Hold a buttercup under your chin and look for a shine, to prove you like butter. "He loves me, he loves me not"—the answer is in the white petals of a daisy. Your worst enemy might find a prickly burr creeping up inside his sleeve; and who put it there? In early spring, we gathered violets, wrapped in leaves and tied with a piece of string, to sell for a nickel on the street corner. One Christmas, I was given a flower press in which to preserve garden and field flowers, which eventually became framed gifts under glass. Do little girls still have such hobbies? Do boys still stretch a blade of grass between their index fingers to use as an earsplitting whistle? Queen Anne's lace is one of the most beautiful blossoms. I let carrots go to seed in the garden to have lacey blooms for bouquets.

We need wildflowers to make a wreath for a little head of curls, or a necklace. One can buy "Meadow in a Can"—seventeen kinds of wildflower seeds to sow, if you have a can opener. But they won't grow in a garden. Only birds, wind, and critters can make a meadow. We must not blow the leaves from under garden bushes. We must allow the highway median to bloom. It seems to me the whole human race is like little children: first, we must try to see if it hurts before we learn not to do it again. We play with space toys, and not until seven brave explorers are lost do we admit to dangers known of since 1981. Will the whole family of man have to face certain extinction—all five billion of us—before we will acknowledge what we already know: that pollution raises atmospheric temperature, higher in the next fifteen years than ever before! An agricultural wasteland is predicted by a few grown-ups, called by some "Nervous Nellies of the Environment."

Reach Out and Touch

The first time I flew in a small, private aircraft, I felt very apprehensive. Whatever other chic forms of transportation I have enjoyed, this is, by far, the most glamorous. Private airports and terminals have a kind of elegant decadence, though often they are not in the least luxurious. Most sleek little planes that flit across the continent for the convenience of chairmen of the board, chief executive officers, and their cohorts often, too often, fly empty or only partially occupied. This fact became a battle cry to action for Priscilla Blum and Jay Weinberg. Both had needed frequent transportation when they were recovering from cancer. Trips to the cancer center for treatment were arduous and expensive. They realized that many people who lived great distances from treatment centers were at a loss about how to get there.

Corporate Angel Network was the answer to the transportation problems for cancer patients who needed periodic treatment, available only at large medical facilities. CAN is headquartered in White Plains, New York, and now has over four hundred participating corporations (even labor unions), putting more than eight hundred aircraft at their disposal. The use of empty seats on already scheduled flights for these patients (and, sometimes, accompanying family members) is provided at no cost to the passengers and creates no expense to the corporation. As President Reagan said in 1984, "The American people have developed a new way of thinking about how to solve social and economic problems. Everywhere you look, people are finding creative solutions to local needs. . . . No bureaucrats involved. Just the people doing it."

*   *   *

Charity is usually somewhat parochial. Each donation is directed toward a recipient whose credo concurs with our own. We give money, goods, time, or talent and—be it for religious, fraternal, political, or an individual's benefit—we choose those that are closest to our own beliefs. Not always, of course, but mostly. Yet not everyone is that way. One outstanding philanthropist is the self-described peace crusader Abie Nathan. Not unlike Don Quixote, he rides not a tired old horse but an equally tired old ship. He has been involved in peace campaigns and in relief efforts in Ethiopia, Nigeria, Nicaragua, and Colombia. An immigrant to Israel, Nathan became a successful restaurateur. When his frustrations with Middle East troubles overshadowed his drive for personal gain, he sold his restaurant and bought the ship. For many decades, he maintained this floating radio station in a one-man campaign to make the Israelis and Arabs understand each other. Long before there was any civil dialogue in that explosive corner of the world, he communicated with both sides from his peace ship in the Mediterranean. He also helped the Colombian people, whose worldly goods were swept away by volcanic eruptions. On his way home from there, he passed through New York. There, he heard about a despicable robbery at St. Patrick's Cathedral, of a poor box, votive candles, and collection plate donations. To voice his outrage, he donated $7,000. He was repaying an ancient debt to the Catholic

Church and to the Jesuits, who had educated him in a
boarding school in India.

* * *

It is possible to run a multimillion-dollar enterprise from
a one-room office with the aid of one single, paid employee.
But, you have to have vision and unbelievable determination, like Robert C. Macauley, who runs a charitable venture
as a sideline to his very profitable paper-manufacturing
business. His one-room operation is called Americares and
deals exclusively with procuring, transporting, and distrib-
uting medical supplies to strife-torn nations. These million-
dollar airlifts contain drugs and pharmaceuticals that have
either been contributed without cost or are paid for by
contributions from Macauley's wealthy friends. "When you
give a dollar to most charities," he says, "only sixty-five or
seventy cents are left after deductions for their bloated bu-
reaucracies and big buildings." Americares has neither bu-
reaucracy nor buildings. "Everything is donated, the office,
the phone, the drugs, the volunteers' time. So I can guarantee that for every dollar donated, not less than twenty-five
dollars' worth of medicine will go to wherever we can save
lives." Sad to say, this moment in history does not lack spots
on earth where such highly organized devotion can find a
target: Poland, Pakistan, Lebanon, Afghanistan, Ethiopia,
Central America, and other sites of strife around the world.
Americares first determines just exactly what is needed and
then makes absolutely sure that distribution is not diverted
by profiteers, military, corrupt officials, or black-market
channels, but reaches the civilian population for which it is
intended.

Macauley hopes that government agencies and other relief organizations will follow his example. He is a very per-
suasive man, who manages to involve just about anyone and
any corporation he sets his sight on in his humanitarian
efforts to help victims of senseless devastation and neglect.

Not all his generosity is exported. Reverend Bruce Rit-

ter's Covenant House in New York—a crisis center for run-
away children—is his special project this side of the ocean.

*   *   *

For families who are poor, evicted, or burned out of their
homes, old hotels in urban areas become home, if one can
call them that. The children, if they go to school at all, are
constantly assigned to a different one each time the family is
relocated. Hardly a situation for learning or improving
themselves enough to climb out of their apparently predes-
tined condition. One small island of hope is the Boys Brotherhood Republic, in New York City, which calls itself the
"World's Smallest Democracy"—a "citizen state" populated by boys aged twelve to twenty. Its history goes back to
Chicago and Jack London, the author, who started Boys'
Brotherhood Republic in 1914. Fiorello LaGuardia brought
it to New York in 1932, to help youngsters who were veering
in the wrong direction due to the effects of the Depression.

Boys will not break the rules if they are given the opportunity to make the rules. Over 1,100 young people are "citizens," some of whom are mentally or physically handi-
capped. The Vincent Astor Foundation built them a fine
building on the Lower East Side, a far cry from the dilapi-
dated tenements to which the children return in the evening. Here, there are no graffiti, no broken windows, no
initials carved into desks. Self-respect is tied to the spotless
maintenance. Self-reliance through self-government. Infractions are handled by their own "police," who bring the
culprits before the "judge"—elected by the boys and a jury
of fellow "citizens." This is not a club but their own country,
in which they prepare themselves for accepting their roles
as American citizens. They learn what makes a society work
—absolute cooperation on the part of each member.

*   *   *

Have you heard of "Hollywood Calls"? It is an organization of famous folks from movieland who use their influence
for the benefit of others. This is not just more of the same

telethon super-specials, personal bravado, or visiting the troops in faraway places. This is just talking on the telephone to an ordinary family or individual with a problem. No speech from a dais, no electronic scoreboard for toting up dollars pledged to a good cause. Some of the actors and actresses who participate in "Hollywood Calls" devote as much as three hours a day making calls to strangers. Do actors know more than psychiatrists? No. But they are trained to feel their way into another's psyche and, perhaps, that is why a personal problem can be talked out successfully with a Hollywood idol.

* * *

It is a tradition among bartenders and barbers to offer their patients a sounding board. They provide a place where a man can hear himself complain—about the boss, the wife, the government; a place to air grievances and be assured that a sympathetic audience of one will commiserate, or better yet, will come up with a word of advice, caution, or encouragement. One man has had the imagination to extend this idea into another aspect of everyday need: professional legal advice, in capsule form. This real estate lawyer runs a hot dog stand in Los Angeles. On Wednesday nights, patrons can go to the back of the stand and get free legal advice with a purchase of a hot dog. It's a community service. Kim Pearlman, Esq., believes it is a way of getting people attuned to the legal system. His plain and garnished hot dogs sell like hotcakes, especially the one with relish, called "Police Dog."

* * *

In 1948, a small group of dedicated professionals and celebrities in the communication arts, sports, and politics created the Veterans Bedside Network. On their weekly visits to veterans' hospitals in the New York area, they bring scripts, sound effects, music, tape recorders, and video cameras. Under their guidance and gentle prodding, hospitalized veterans become actors. This is involvement therapy for patients, whose mental, emotional, or physical condition confines them—each to his own world of isolation or alienation. Rather than bringing entertainment *to* them, Bedside Network draws out their inner resources, their strengths and talents. Miracles happen, literally in front of your eyes. The program has now expanded to five other cities. Week after week, hospitalized veterans are visited by these itinerant play troupes, honoring them with personal involvement.

* * *

Networks are being formed in most communities, staffed by paraprofessionals who stand by, twenty-four hours a day, to provide information, referrals, and counseling for many types of emergencies. The Kiwanis Club, for example, has a toll-free Drug and Alcoholism hot line. Most parents of children with drug-related problems are beside themselves with fear, shame, confusion, and hopelessness. They have no knowledge about where to turn for help. Referring the caller to the right agency is of immediate and immeasurable value. Often, it is a child who calls, and the telephone volunteer is a rehabilitated drug abuser who has personally benefited from similar programs during recovery. There are other networks that connect troubled people to agencies for legal advice, emergency food, medical care, temporary housing. Some who call are depressed or suicidal. Others want to get help for a relative or friend. Sometimes, it is just a question of information or a sympathetic ear. Whatever the problem—family feud, sexual concern—the response is always nonjudgmental. No sermons, no threats, no "If I were you . . ." or "the same thing happened to me . . ." No one will make light of the problem, be critical or harsh.

Person-to-person outreach—there is always need for another hand.

* * *

Not everyone who needs help teeters at the edge of an abyss. Patrons of the arts sometimes become patients of the

arts. Most theatergoers have a tradition of making it "a
night on the town": drinks, dinner, theater, late hours. Too
often, it means rushing and excitement; drinking too fast,
eating too much, hurrying to make the curtain. No wonder,
then, that the question "Is there a doctor in the house?" is
not always comic horseplay. But, is there a doctor in the
house? At the Lincoln Center complex in New York, you can
be sure of it. A sufficient number of young residents from
nearby Roosevelt Hospital make it their voluntary duty to
appear at least once a week for a pair of free tickets. In
exchange, they are on call during the performance to minister to the emergency needs of theatergoers. Almost every
evening or matinee there is need for a doctor. Sometimes it
is nothing more serious than an ankle turned on the stair-
case or a finger caught in a door. Other times, a wolfed-
down dinner causes enough discomfort to frighten someone into an imagined heart attack. A cocktail too many,
imbibed on an empty stomach, will keep the on-duty MDs
busy when they might have preferred the onstage performance. Preexisting disabilities can surface when least expected. Sometimes the mere thought of disturbing others
or being unable to leave triggers a faint or panic. Claustro-
phobia can take on monumental proportions for one who is
susceptible and not seated on the aisle.

Doctors who are in private practice are not allowed to
sign up for duty at Lincoln Center, because it is considered
an opportunity for resident doctors to enjoy the arts. The
most coveted nights to be on duty at the Opera House are,
of course, Mondays, when most openings take place and the
audience is especially elegant. Matinees may keep the young
doctor busier than he or she would like. It is then that many
older people come to the theater, and children, who are just
as likely to need medical care.

Kim Stanley and I played together in *Touch of the Poet* when
she was very young, terribly nervous, and quite neurotic.
She has been credited with missing more performances
than any actress. Her life seems to have been one long
nightmare; so was working with her. During one intermis-

sion she decided that she could not go on; the audience was
to be sent home. So the manager went out to ask if there was
a doctor in the house. And who should come backstage to
minister to this unworthy somatizing young woman but Dr.
Jonas Salk, the distinguished discoverer of the polio vaccine.

* * *

And I continue to flit around the country. No longer one-
nighters and rooming houses, as in the early days, but often
one-day visits to a friend who is ill or lonely or to make brief
speeches from a dais for causes that attract my support.
Would I rather stay home? Of course; I say that every day.
The world can do it without me. But I have never quite
mastered the part of bystander. The flight attendant who
punched my New York–Washington ticket into the computer for the third time in one week put it quite bluntly:
"Not again, Miss Hayes!"